Retah Mcpherson

Going Deeper

An inspirational journey to deepen
your relationship with the Father, Son & Spirit

© Retah McPherson

ISBN 978-0-9922238-7-8

© All rights reserved.
No part of this book may be reproduced or transmitted in any form or by any means; electronic or
mechanical, including photocopying and recording,
or by any information storage or retrieval system,
except as my be expressly permitted in writing by the publisher.

Scripture quotations are taken from:
The New King James Version® (NKJV) Copyright © 1982
by Thomas Nelson, Inc.
The Amplified® Bible (AMP) Copyright © 1954, 1962, 1965, 1987
by The Lockman Foundation.
The Amplified Bible Classic Edition® (AMPC) Copyright © 2015
by The Lockman Foundation.
All rights reserved.
Scripture quotations noted KJV are from the King James Version of the Bible.

Cover photograph: Claudia De Nobrega (www.claudiadenobrega.com)
Hair & Makeup: Marli Basson (www.marlibasson.co.za)
Compilation: Noeline N. Neumann (Noeline.Neumann@gmail.com)
Cover design & Layout: Cilmi Steyn (cm.steyn@telkomsa.net)

McPherson House
P.O. Box 632
Stellenbosch
7599
South Africa
Tel: +27 (0) 82 610 5757
www.retahmcpherson.com

First edition, first print 2015

Going Deeper

Preface   5

Going deeper   8

Examine your heart   36

Receive your healing   64

Spiritual warfare—Fight the battle   92

Renew your mind   120

Finding your true identity   148

Kingdom Living   176

Walking in Truth and Light   204

Living in YHVH's presence   232

Walking by Faith   260

Preface

Along the journey of life our Abba Father constantly teaches us through the trails and tests in our lives. He gives us a hunger to know Him better, and this hunger takes us deeper and deeper into His heart. There we learn to know Him and trust Him more. By exercising our faith in Him our "faith muscles" are developed and they become stronger for whatever we face on our journey.

As we explore deeper into YHVH's heart we experience how much He loves and cares for us. We learn that He is always there for us and we start to know His nature. The beauty of the journey is that the closer we come to Him the more we are changed into His likeness.

This journal contains some of the faith nuggets Abba Father has taught me over the years.

YHVH is real, and He is faithful. He knows everything about you and even in your darkest moment He is with you. He longs for you to have an intimate, passionate love relationship with him. This oneness is one of the greatest gifts that He has given you as His child.

I hope that–
- you will allow Holy Spirit to go deep in your heart, so that you can receive healing through YHVH's love
- you will be hungry enough to ask for His Holy Fire inside your spirit to continually burn and take you deep into the Father's heart.

Speak to Holy Spirit while you make your way through the lessons in this book and receive His love and mercy in your life.

What you will find deep in His heart is—love—unconditional love for you! It is the place where He teaches you how to forgive, how to serve and above all—how to love!

Love is the language of Truth, and Truth sets us free!

I pray that you will be enriched as you take this journey of Going Deeper.

Retah

How to use these inspirational messages:

These inspirational messages are all about Going Deeper with God. If you are holding this book in your hand then Holy Spirit has spoken to your spirit through the title. You want to go deeper with God.

Through this series of inspirational themes and messages you will embark on a journey with Holy Spirit that will take you deeper in your relationship with God, the Father and Yeshua, His Son.

In order to get the most out of this experience I suggest that you do the following:

- Take the time to reflect upon the Scripture and the message.
- Allow yourself the space to be quiet before the Father. It is in the quiet that Holy Spirit will be able to communicate with you.
- Then use either the space below each message or your prayer journal to record what Holy Spirit says to you.

How lovely is your dwelling place,
Lord Almighty!
My soul yearns, even faints,
for the courts of the Lord;
my heart and my flesh cry out
for the living God.
Even the sparrow has found a home,
and the swallow a nest for herself,
where she may have her young—
a place near your altar,
Lord Almighty, my King and my God.
Blessed are those who dwell in your house;
they are ever praising you.
Psalm 84:1-4

Going Deeper

My soul yearns for you in the night;
in the morning my spirit longs for you.
When your judgments come upon the earth,
the people of the world learn righteousness.
Isaiah 26:9

The journey begins...

Do not be conformed to this world (this age), [fashioned after and adapted to its external, superficial customs], but be transformed (changed) by the [entire] renewal of your mind [by its new ideals and its new attitude], so that you may prove [for yourselves] what is the good and acceptable and perfect will of God, even the thing which is good and acceptable and perfect [in His sight for you].
Romans 12:2 [AMPLIFIED BIBLE]

God walks with us step by step. It is a daily walk, seeking to go deeper with God. It is a journey, a mountain to climb—but, let me tell you, it is the best journey I have ever been on, because I am NEVER alone! We are all in a sanctification process—for the redemption of our souls. The renewing of our minds is a key element in this process. Much is spoken and written about it, but few people live it. We must be completely committed to the sanctification process, co-operating with YHVH not resisting Him.

We learn to know God's good, acceptable and perfect will by renewing our minds. As our minds become renewed—we begin to think more like God. This is part of the process of going deeper with Him. Instead of a selfish and self-centred agenda, we have His mind. As we go deeper we learn to listen to the voice of Holy Spirit and we start to know His heart for us. He shares how He wants us to pray, where He wants us to go and what He wants us to do. When this happens we can begin to move in His good, acceptable, and perfect will for us. Step by step He will lead us deeper. It is there that you will find peace of heart and mind.

Reflection:
*   As you read the Scripture once again what is God saying to you?
*   Do you choose the Spirit or the flesh today?

Response:
Spend some time reflecting and then writing what Holy Spirit says to you.

I want more of Him!

The Lord replied, "My Presence will go with you, and I will give you rest." Then Moses said to him, "If your Presence does not go with us, do not send us up from here." And the Lord said to Moses, "I will do the very thing you have asked, because I am pleased with you and I know you by name." Then Moses said, "Now show me your glory."
Exodus 33:14-15, 17-18

I hear the same cry all over the world: "I want more of Him—more of the King. I want to hear His voice!" This is revival! It makes me so excited because we are called to develop an ever deepening love relationship with our King. I can hear people's anger because YHVH doesn't give them what they ask for. There are people who want the blessing but they ask out of self-righteousness. It is not about what we have or don't have, no, it is all about Him. Only in Him is there perfect peace!

Within our DNA YHVH has designed an insatiable hunger for communion with Him. It is a hunger to know Him more intimately—as your Abba Father—the One who loves us and cares for us. He wants to progressively reveal Himself, His will, and His ways to us—all in His perfect time. The more time we spend with Him the better we get to know Him. And here, He chooses the timing, the nature, the substance of all the interactions that lead us into a deeper relationship and revelations of Yeshua. Holy Spirit is in us and we need to come to the place where we don't take a step without Him. A place, where we know, that our thoughts are as loud as our words to Yeshua.

Reflection:
* How do you know YHVH—intellectually or experientially?
* Where you are in your life right now—are you at peace with waiting for His timing?

Response:
What is Holy Spirit saying to you today—take time to wait on Him and then to write down what He says to you.

Laying down your life

*If you do whatever I command you and walk in obedience to me and do
what is right in my eyes by obeying my decrees and commands.*
1 Kings 11:38a

Yeshua is waiting for you to lay down your life—not to hold on to it. That means trusting in Him alone and following wherever He leads. I have to allow Him to burn all the sin out of my life and to cleanse me as deep as my DNA—through the Blood of the Lamb. There is a remnant yearning for holiness, not legalism, examining their hearts and having a desire to obey the voice of Holy Spirit implicitly. Do you identify with the remnant in our day? Is your heart broken over the condition of your own soul, your children's lives, your family's lives, the condition of your city and your country? Do you find yourself weeping and crying to YHVH just like Daniel and Nehemiah did for revival in your life? Are you looked upon as "peculiar" by Christians who do not share these feelings?

If you answered yes to these questions then take courage, you are part of YVHV's remnant that He is raising up. Take up your position and let His refining fire do its work to make you a pure and humble vessel. I am more and more content—wanting to obey His voice. Knowing that I can do nothing in my own strength. All I know is that I want to live in His revelation and not human knowledge.

Reflection:
* Do you yearn to walk in holiness and power?
* The path to living in this way is through laying down your life.

Response:
Are you at the place where you are ready to lay down your life?
Talk to Holy Spirit about this.

Abide in Me

"I am the vine, you are the branches. He who abides in Me, and I in him,
bears much fruit; for without Me you can do nothing."
John 15:5 [NEW KING JAMES VERSION]

The reason that we go through trials every day is that we are being prepared to be the remnant, the overcomers. You cannot learn this from books, only through practical trials and tests. The God whom we serve is faithful and full of wisdom! He said to me: "Retah, I want you to view trials as exercises designed to develop your trust, obedience and surrender-muscles. You live in the midst of fierce spiritual battles, and "fear" is one of Satan's favorite weapons. My child, when "fear" speaks to you, immediately affirm your trust in Me. Don't allow those voices to manipulate you. Start to train your spirit to speak the Word out loud. Abide in Me, don't do anything without Me, and allow My Holy Spirit to speak to you.

"Stay in a love relationship with Me. That means communicating with Me all the time in the Spirit. RESIST the Devil in My Name, stay in Truth, stay in the Light and be transparent. Keep your thoughts in the Light and be on the lookout for the voice of Jezebel that would do anything to draw you back into old patterns. Don't look back My child, yesterday is gone. I want you to focus on today. Be "now-conscious." So many people are stuck in the past, or are dreaming about their life in the future, but are afraid of today."

Reflection:

* Are you fearful—if so what are you afraid of?
* What does it mean to be "now-conscious?"

Response:

Ask Holy Spirit to reveal to you what YHVH wants you to learn today.

Stay in the Light

*But if we walk in the light, as he is in the light, we have fellowship with one another,
and the blood of Jesus, his Son, purifies us from all sin.*
1 John 1:7

One of the greatest things we have learned is the power of the Glory Light of Yeshua. Whenever I pray the Glory Light, I can see things are happening because where there was darkness Yeshua's Light and Truth shines into our souls. The lies of the enemy are exposed and the Truth alone sets us free.

To walk in the Light means that we hide nothing from YHVH. We tell Him everything in our hearts. We invite Him into our pain. The first step towards a love relationship is honesty. Yeshua spoke more against hypocrites than anything else. Yeshua asks us to be transparent not perfect. We must take responsibility and be honest. The first step is to immediately confess my sins to YHVH, calling them by name. "Lord, I repent of the iniquity, transgressions and rebellion of the same sin in my DNA, I cut myself loose from any curses or words spoken over me (bewitchment) in Yeshua's Name." Take responsibility for your actions, take up your position in Christ, repent, apply the blood of the Lamb and be set free. Holy Spirit will guide you into all truth. The more darkness dwells in your heart: Hidden sin, anger and unforgiveness, the less you will hear His voice. Don't use the excuse, "God knows my heart." No, take responsibility and leave your old ways behind.

Reflection:
*   What are you not taking responsibility for?
*   How transparent are you?

Response:
Spend time in Holy Spirit's presence.
Ask Him to show you where you are not being transparent.

The beauty of holiness

Whoever conceals their sins does not prosper,
but the one who confesses and renources them finds mercy.
Proverbs 28:13

Yeshua is looking for something specific in His Bride—"the beauty of holiness." Holiness is the antitheses of sin, which is unfaithfulness toward YHVH. There is no such thing as a big sin or a small sin. Sin is sin and it affects the condition of our hearts. The beauty of holiness is real and genuine, and therefore it differs radically from the world's perception or definition of beauty. Even when physical beauty is natural it is rarely accompanied by the inner beauty of the love of Yeshua that flows from the heart.

I spoke to someone who participates in the Mrs. South Africa pageant. She said, "People will do anything to win that crown." "You know, I can only tell you that ten years ago when I entered my heart was empty and dark. I believed the crown would fill some of the darkness in me. But that night after winning I walked into the hotel room with the crown on my head, and nothing had changed in my heart. I sat down and wept. Then I went on my face, I took the crown off and handed it to Yeshua, saying, 'Lord, nothing has changed in my heart, please take this crown and exchange it for the Crown of Life (the Crown of the Overcomer).' I wiped my tears, stood up, not realizing the journey that lay before me."

Reflection:
* What are you using to try and fill the dark holes in your heart?
* Have you come to the place yet where you realize that only Yeshua can fill the holes?

Response:
Lay your crown before Him and ask Him to exchange it for the Crown of the Overcomer.

The Light of the world

When Jesus spoke again to the people, he said, "I am the light of the world. Whoever follows me will never walk in darkness, but will have the light of life."
John 8:12

My life has radically changed over the past ten years. Today I run the race of life—in the Light of Yeshua. The reason I run this race is to receive the Crown of Life. The wonderful thing is that no man can ever take this crown away from me. It is a crown that belongs to everyone who overcomes. So let's not run after fame, riches, and all the things that this world offers us. Let us rather choose to remain in the Light of Yeshua's love.

The beauty of holiness is abiding, it is satisfying, and therefore differs radically from the beauty of the temporal or the sensual. There is more to mankind than the material, therefore they require something besides material things, no matter how beautiful, to meet their needs. It is the things of Holy Spirit alone that brings satisfaction. But godliness with contentment is great gain (1 Timothy 6:6). We need to have a greater thirst for righteousness than we do for satisfying self. The true beauty of Holiness is to glorify YHVH in everything that we do. *Oh, worship the Lord in the beauty of holiness!* (Psalm 96:9a NEW KING JAMES VERSION). This is the only kind of beauty Yeshua cares about in our devotions. Godliness is to the soul as light is to the world.

Reflection:
*   Truthfully, what would you rather have: An earthly crown or the Crown of Life?
*   Are there things that you are trying to use to fill your needs?

Response:
Oh, worship the Lord in the beauty of holiness! Spend time worshipping before Yeshua.

New Life

Therefore, if anyone is in Christ, the new creation has come:
The old has gone, the new is here!
2 Corinthians 5:17

In this new life you will receive and experience a new way of living in and through Yeshua:
- New eyes: To see people as Yeshua sees them; you will see the condition of their heart.
- New ears: To hear God's voice clearly; so that you can immediately obey His voice.
- New tongue: To sing forth the praises of YHVH instead of speaking death, gossip, murmuring, slander and backbiting. Not to speak self-pity, but rather to thank Yeshua in everything you do.
- New nose: To breathe the fragrance of obedience, and not the filth of compromise.
- New hands: To lift up holy hands, praising Yeshua. He who has clean hands can enter into the holy tabernacle of YHVH.
- New legs: To take the Gospel of Peace everywhere. To run the race of faith instead of a race that is all about self.

Being transformed into the likeness of Yeshua, is a daily process. He asks for us to be holy, to be set apart. Not many are willing to say "Lord, I will give my life to honor You, to obey You, to become like You and to carry Your likeness, all for Your glory." Sin has caused us to lose the glory of YHVH. So being born again means to be begotten of Yeshua. The children of YHVH will manifest His glory.

Reflection:
- Go through each of the gifts of new life in Yeshua.
- Ask Holy Spirit to show you whether you are living out this new life fully.

Response:
Write down what He shows you and what He says to you.

____

____

____

____

____

____

____

____

Doing His will

Teach me to do Your will, for You are my God; Your Spirit is good.
Lead me in the land of uprightness.
Psalm 143:10 [NEW KING JAMES VERSION]

We are all on a journey to overcome the brokenness and sin in our souls. If we want to go deeper with YHVH, deeper with Yeshua and deeper with Holy Spirit then we need to walk in obedience. David wrote: *Teach me to do Your will...* Yeshua has paid the full price for us to become whole. But, we also have a responsibility. How will I be set free from a soul that is characterized by spiritual death? The sin that lives in my soul has been imparted since the fall of man, and it brings spiritual death. The purpose of the sin is to separate us from this one thing... an intimate love relationship with Yeshua.

The greatest battle that we face is the salvation of our souls. This is why the Psalmist said: *Lead me in the land of uprightness.* Paul appeals for the deliverance of his soul. He asks to be freed from the spiritual opposition working against the true desire of his heart. It is the same with all of us. We battle against our fallen nature, the parts of us that are still characterized by spiritual death. If we are serious about going deeper with God we have to realize that the key is to make the right choices. We are what we choose. Therefore, our choices are vitally important.

Reflection:

- What are the choices that you are making on a daily basis? Are they leading you into a deeper relationship with YHVH?
- If this is not the case then what are you going to do about it?

Response:

Pray the Psalmist's prayer: *Teach me to do Your will, for You are my God; Your Spirit is good. Lead me in the land of uprightness.*

Bear fruit with patience

YHVH's Spirit lives in the heart of man. Both Heaven and earth meet in the heart of mankind. The pure heart of man is like a fruitful garden. It receives spiritual seed from YHVH and grows into the natural world so that it will be visible for all to see. The soil must be moistened and protected by the life-giving, brooding care of Holy Spirit. If we love Yeshua we will have an intimate relationship with Him, we will receive His seed and become pregnant with His plans for our lives. If we, however, love another god as well, we will have mixed seed inside of us. Mixed seed will never produce the pure fruit we want and will keep us from entering into YHVH's perfect destiny for our lives.

We cannot change our actions or character by trying harder to be a good person. No, we must change our belief system. Patience is required to reap a harvest. This is the most difficult part for all of us. There is a period of time between the planting and the production. Our part is to patiently wait for the harvest, taking care of the soil and the growing seeds or plants. Yeshua by His Spirit brings growth, but we have to provide a proper atmosphere, nutrients and care for the plants.

Reflection:

- Have you ever thought of your heart as a fruitful garden?
- Ask Holy Spirit to shine Yeshua's Glory Light into your heart so that you can see what is growing there.

Response:

Write down what Holy Spirit shows you and then bring it before YHVH.

Maintain the unity

Every time a husband and a wife fight they open the spiritual portal for Satan to send his demons to attack them and their family. When we fight we create an atmosphere in which the evil one thrives. On the other hand when you resist the temptation to react in the flesh and instead react out of YHVH's love you will be able to be patient and long suffering. His love opens the spiritual portal for Holy Spirit to pour out the dew of His love, causing the seed of faith to grow until the plant becomes visible.

Many people ask why it takes such a long time. You have to remember the process that a seed goes through. It will take as long as it takes for us to begin living in the atmosphere of faith—with a heart fully trusting Yeshua. This means that you must hold on to the Word or vision that Holy Spirit planted into your heart, even when you cannot see anything with your natural eye. You will lose your vision if you abandon it in your heart. Many worthy works for YHVH, planted in the heart of man, have failed to come to fruition because the "seed" was abandoned. It is the same as when a brooding hen leaves the nest one day to soon, all the eggs will come to nothing.

Reflection:

- Are you allowing friction and strife in your home to open the portal for Satan to enter?
- Is the vision that YHVH has given you in danger of dying because of lack of care and perseverance?

Response:

What are you going to do about the state of your heart?

Producing many seeds

Very truly I tell you, unless a kernel of wheat falls to the ground and dies,
it remains only a single seed. But if it dies, it produces many seeds.
John 12:24

Take care of the soil of your heart and keep it loose. Don't allow your heart to become hardened because seed cannot grow in a hard heart. Keep it tender with forgiveness, love, mercy, kindness, and patience. Be ruthless in keeping out the weeds of useless and cursed words, negative or fearful thoughts such as, "you cannot do this." Thoughts like these steal the nutrition from the seeds in your heart.

Trimming and pruning is always part of the growth process, don't sulk when you are being pruned. James tells us to, *Consider it pure joy, - whenever you face trials of many kinds* (1:2). When we pray and meditate on Yeshua's Word we experience the spiritual realm in the natural. This happens when I am in a place of inner quietness seeking His presence. I believe with all my heart that YHVH will finish what He has started in our lives. We will walk this journey to the end and we will be overcomers, the Remnant of Christ. I believe that His plans are plans for good, not evil (Jeremiah 29:11). YHVH is not a man that He can lie (Numbers 23:19). I believe that our job in this process is to keep the weeds out, to clean the soil and to live a life in Him. This is our journey of faith.

Reflection:
* What are you doing to actively keep the weeds out of your heart?
* What are the negative thoughts that you are allowing to pop into your mind?

Response:
Write a list of what you believe in the light of what Holy Spirit has shown you.

The True Light

When Jesus spoke again to the people, he said, "I am the light of the world.
Whoever follows me will never walk in darkness, but will have the light of life."
John 8:12

The tabernacle that is described in the book of Exodus amongst other places also depicts us. Our inner man or soul is the part of the tabernacle that is the Holy Place. And the Holy of Holies is our spirit. The outer court corresponds to our physical bodies. The Holy Place and our soul are illuminated by the seven branched lamp stand. The only sources of light for the Holy of Holies and our spirit is the presence of YHVH.

What we learn from this is that our inner man has a spiritual lampstand with seven branches. These correspond to the lampstand found in the tabernacle. When we are still living in flesh, in our fallen-nature condition, our lampstand is lit by the darkness of the flesh. It operates under sin and it illuminates our beings with "dark light" or false light. In this state you believe that what you are doing is right. You are living in denial because you cannot see what Yeshua sees. You are filled with darkness. But, unaware of this, you continue believing that you are always right. In the restoration process of our inner man the lampstand undergoes a process whereby the "dark light" is replaced by the True Light of Yeshua—the seven fold spirit of YHVH. If we follow Him we will not walk in darkness.

Reflection:
- Who is illuminating your lampstand?
- Are you living in denial believing that what you are doing is right?

Response:
Ask Holy Spirit to light your lampstand with the True Light.

The sanctification process

"The eye is the lamp of the body. If your eyes are healthy, your whole body will be full of light. But if your eyes are unhealthy, your whole body will be full of darkness. If then the light within you is darkness, how great is that darkness!"
Mathew 6:22-23

There is a process involved in our sanctification. It will never happen instantaneously or over a short period of time. It is a journey that we have to walk. Moment by moment and day by day. Then Jesus said to His disciples, *"If anyone wishes to follow Me [as My disciple], he must deny himself [set aside selfish interests], and take up his cross [expressing a willingness to endure whatever may come] and follow Me [believing in Me, conforming to My example in living and, if need be, suffering or perhaps dying because of faith in Me]. For whoever wishes to save his life [in this world] will [eventually] lose it [through death], but whoever loses his life [in this world] for My sake will find it [that is, life with Me for all eternity]"* (Mathew 16:24-25 AMPLIFIED BIBLE).

It all starts with a passionate desire to follow Yeshua with everything inside of us. The old man must die. You have to deny yourself, take up your cross and obey Yeshua even to the point of losing your life. This is how the light is replaced in our lampstand from the light of darkness to the Light of Yeshua. The "dark light" are our flesh, our mind, the world, sins and lusts of the flesh. This is our condition before the Light who is Yeshua comes into our lives.

Reflection:
* Have you become impatient with your sanctification process?
* How is this affecting your life?

Response:
Recommit yourself to walking the sanctification walk, one day at a time with Yeshua.

The Spirit of the Lord

The Spirit of the Lord will rest on him—the Spirit of wisdom and of understanding, the Spirit of counsel and of might, the Spirit of the knowledge and fear of the Lord—
Isaiah 11:2

This a description of us before Yeshua saved us: *As for you, you were dead in your transgressions and sins, in which you used to live when you followed the ways of this world and of the ruler of the kingdom of the air, the spirit who is now at work in those who are disobedient. All of us also lived among them at one time, gratifying the cravings of our flesh and following its desires and thoughts. Like the rest, we were by nature deserving of wrath* (Ephesians 2:1-3). As we surrender everything to Yeshua, yielding more and more to His process of restoration, His seven-fold Spirit will start flowing through us.

The Spirit of the Lord is made up of seven spirits, but we only see and speak of One. In the same way that natural light is one, but when it passes through a prism, it displays the seven colors of the rainbow, so is Holy Spirit. When we speak to one another we can discern and even hear which spirit is talking. Is it the light of darkness (false light that has the correct language but no power?) or the True Light of YHVH? The light from YHVH's lampstand illuminates our entire beings resulting in changed motives, mind-sets, beliefs, fears, attitudes and the way we live our daily lives.

Reflection:
- Spend some time allowing Holy Spirit to examine your motives, mind-sets, beliefs, fears and attitudes. How are you living your life?
- What does this tell you?

Response:
Ask Holy Spirit to lead you into all Truth so that you can have the True Light shining in your life.

True Light vs. false light

The "dark light" will always manifest in you in these ways: *But if you have bitter jealousy and selfish ambition in your hearts, do not be arrogant, and [as a result] be in defiance of the truth. This [superficial] wisdom is not that which comes down from above, but is earthly (secular), natural (unspiritual), even demonic. For where jealousy and selfish ambition exist, there is disorder [unrest, rebellion] and every evil thing and morally degrading practice.* (James 3:14-16 AMPLIFIED BIBLE).

On the other hand James 3:17 tells us that when we have Yeshua's True Light shining in us we will have *...the wisdom from above which is first pure [morally and spiritually undefiled], then peace-loving [courteous, considerate], gentle, reasonable [and willing to listen], full of compassion and good fruits. It is unwavering, without [self-righteous] hypocrisy [and self-serving guile].* As Yeshua's Light starts to replace the false light in us, we begin to manifest the character of Christ in and through us. Only Yeshua's Light can lift the veil of denial. I was in denial for such a long time in my life. Today, I praise YHVH for our journey of faith that opened my eyes to all the veils of denial I lived under. Yes, the fire of YHVH burned those veils away and we could begin discerning what was truth and what was false.

Reflection:

* Have another look at James 3:14-16 and James 3:17. Which of the lists of characteristics applies to your life?
* Ask Holy Spirit for discernment to be able to distinguish the true from the false.

Response:

Ask Yeshua to shine His Glory Light into all the dark places in your life.

His hands and feet

*My prayer is not that you take them out of the world
but that you protect them from the evil one.*
John 17:15

YHVH is the God of revival. When we are in His presence He reveals more of Himself to us. He is the life-giving God who brings the spiritually dead back to life. He is the Resurrection, and the River of Life. He does the work but we are His hands and feet.

When you are one with Him, His presence envelops and infuses you wherever you go. In the morning I say, "Morning Abba Father, morning Yeshua, morning Holy Spirit. I cannot live for one moment without You. I have everything because You are in my life. I have abundance and I can face anything because Christ in me is my hope of Glory! You are truly the treasure of my heart. I thirst for You like a deer thirsts for water. My only rest and peace is in You and You alone. You are my shelter from within. You dwell in the hearts of those who have childlike faith, and have silence within their hearts and live from that place of peace." Confront your daily difficulties out of that place of peace—from the heart of YHVH. As long as we are on this earth we are to serve and be a witness for Yeshua—you cannot do this hiding at home. My friend you cannot renounce the world as long as you are in the world.

Reflection:
- What are your first thoughts and words when you wake up in the morning?
- YHVH has called you to be His witness here on earth—have you embraced His command?

Response:
Write a morning prayer to YHVH telling Him how much you love Him, and committing yourself to be His witness here on earth.

In the world, not of the world

...use the things of the world, as if not engrossed in them.
1 Corinthians 7:31a

YHVH has put us on this earth to live and to engage with the world around us. We are meant to make an impact for Him. We are His hands and His feet! Yeshua's will is that we should use the things of this world in the right way, so that we are preparing a spiritual home for ourselves.

How do I continue to live productively in this world? Through fellowship with YHVH, Yeshua and Holy Spirit. In fellowship with Him we experience peace that is totally unknown to the world. I desire this intimacy more than anything else From this place the world cannot draw me in. Rather I can give to the world from what I have received. I can give because I have Christ in me. I can bring YHVH's Kingdom to my workplace, to the congregation, to the school or university, and wherever I go. More than ever before the body of Christ needs to be so aware of the voices that are out there. Don't be fooled by people's gifts, make sure you see the fruit of Holy Spirit! Let's make sure we bring YHVH's Kingdom to earth and live life to the fullest. Faith is not about hiding, no, faith is trusting YHVH in every situation I face. Faith is having my feet on the ground and living life to the full!

Reflection:
* Have you noticed that many Christians find it hard find a balance between the world and their faith?
* Why do you think this is, and how do you do it?

Response:
Journal your answers to the questions above.

The greatest of these is love

And now these three remain: faith, hope and love.
But the greatest of these is love.
1 Corinthians 13:13

We were created to worship YHVH. Service is an act of worship: Service to YHVH and our fellow man. So let's serve YHVH with all of our heart, soul, mind and strength; and love all those around us as we love ourselves. Then we won't be constantly be thinking about ourselves. Selfishness and self-centredness will flee from our hearts and we will become true sons of YHVH. The time that we spend living in this world is preparation for the future. We are being groomed in the school of the Spirit to face our destiny—and eternity with YHVH. So why would we want to hide from the world? Why would we believe that cutting ourselves off from the world will make us more Spiritual. Yeshua sent His Disciples out into the world to spread the Good News of His Love and Grace.Running the race of life means: **Loving** in spite of not being loved in return.**Giving** without wanting anything in return. **Serving** without being served.**Taking** the Kingdom to a world filled with evil.

You are called to be sons of YHVH. Let the world see and experience His love in you. But for right now, until that completeness, we have three things to do: Trust steadily in God, hope unswervingly, and love extravagantly. And the best of the three is love.

Reflection:
* Did you feel Holy Spirit challenging you as you read this piece today?
* Allow Holy Spirit to speak deeply into your heart and spirit.

Response:
Look again at **Loving, Giving, Serving**, and **Taking**.
Write next to each one how you intend to live out YHVH's commands.

A deepening relationship

YHVH wants us to know Him personally, not to have a second-hand knowledge that comes through someone else. We must have our own intimate love relationship with Him. Yeshua defined Eternal Life as knowing YHVH and Him personally. *And this is eternal life: [it means] to know (to perceive, recognize, become acquainted with, and understand) You, the only true and real God, and [likewise] to know Him, Jesus [as the] Christ (the Anointed One, the Messiah), Whom You have sent* (John 17:3 AMPLIFIED CLASSIC EDITION). If you want to have a relationship like this with Yeshua then you have to surrender everything to Him. You have to listen to Holy Spirit's voice in your life. In order to stay alive our spirits need to drink from His Living water.

We need to listen to and heed every Word that proceeds from YHVH's mouth. His disciples asked Him how? And He answered that sitting at His feet and listening are the most important things you can do in your life. Knowing and loving YHVH every day, in every situation of our lives will make us overcomers. He alone can guide your next step. Only He has all the answers to your questions. We must listen to Him, walk in obedience to Him and ask Him to shine His Glory Light in the dark places in our lives.

Reflection:
* Are you prepared to do what it takes to go deeper with YHVH, Yeshua and Holy Spirit?
* Drinking from the Living Water keeps your spirit alive—when last have you drunk deeply?

Response:
Write a prayer to YHVH expressing your desire to go deeper with Him.

Looking to YHVH

Guide me in your truth and teach me,
for you are God my Savior, and my hope is in you all day long.
Psalm 25:5

By this His Truth will be revealed. And it is only Yeshua's Truth that will set us free. He said: *"I am the way and the truth and the life. No one comes to the Father except through me"* (John 14:6). Too often we run to man instead of to Yeshua. What He does for one He wants to do for all. *You do not have because you do not ask God* (James 4:2c).

Let your spirit be filled with Holy Spirit then you will thirst only after Him, your desire will be for Him. Money will not mean more to you than Yeshua. You will not crave comfort more than Him. You will be content. To hear His voice and to be one with Him will be greater to you than anything else in the world. Those who worship money, ease and convenience will always find something to complain about. You will get to a place where you see YHVH's hand in every situation. You will know and experience His mighty hand in every area of your life. He even turns the bad around for His glory. Finding the Tree of Life (YHVH) will bring you to the place where you are no longer interested in the tree of knowledge of good and evil. The more you look to YHVH, the more you become like Him.

Reflection:

- Are you unhappy? If so is it because you worship money, ease and convenience?
- Going deeper with YHVH means that you look to Him and Him alone for all your needs.

Response:

Spend time telling YHVH how much you long to go deeper with Him.
Ask Him to lead you into His Truth.

Pass on blessings to others

*Surely you have granted him unending blessings
and made him glad with the joy of your presence.*
Psalm 21:6

We can exchange our DNA for Abba's DNA. A friend wrote: 'Retah, the Lord showed me that what you cling to you will pass on to others.' Do you really want to pass on your double life to your children? Your greatest legacy to your family is a DNA washed in Yeshua's Blood. This speaks of a lifestyle where you: Take up your cross and follow Yeshua; you ask Holy Spirit to search your heart; you die to self, and humility comes naturally because you have Yeshua's nature. You will readily ask forgiveness because you know its power, and that your prayers are not acceptable by YHVH if you have wronged anyone—your brother, husband, child, worker, or friend. So, as soon as Holy Spirit reminds you, you leave your gift at the altar and settle the matter with that person first, and then return to offer your gifts to YHVH (Matthew 5:23-24).

You are blessed to be a blessing. Remember to look upward, inward and outward. Because, if you only look upward, you will be unrealistic and of no use in bringing His Kingdom to earth. If you only look inward, you can become discouraged, and if you only look outward you will stay in the shallow waters. But a son of YHVH looks in three directions at all times, because we are body, soul and spirit.

Reflection:
- You are saved in order to be a blessing to your family, your friends, the body of Christ and the world.
- How are you doing in the blessing department?

Response:
Thank Yeshua for His blessings upon your life and ask Him to make you a blessing to all you come in contact with.

Trust in the Lord

Trust in the Lord with all your heart and lean not on your own understanding;
in all your ways submit to him, and he will make your paths straight.
Proverbs 3:5-6

Spending time with the Father, sharing your heart—loving Him, obeying Him, trusting Him—this is how you really learn to know Him. You see, knowing facts about someone, and having an intimate love relationship with someone are two totally different things. You can know the Bible from beginning to end, even understand Greek and Hebrew, and still be spiritually bankrupt if you do not know Yeshua. There was a difference between the disciples and the Pharisees. The difference was that the disciples spent three and a half years with Yeshua. So the key is spending time with Yeshua getting to know Him, because this builds intimacy and trust.

In order to find Life we must come to Him. There are many people who have intellectual knowledge about YHVH, but they're missing the most important thing—experientially KNOWING, LOVING, and TRUSTING YHVH with all their heart, mind, soul and everything in them. It is so easy, you just need to totally surrender to Him, depending only on Yeshua and His will for your life. When problems arise in your life—do you seek mans' counsel or do you first seek YHVH's face? Do you spend your time trying to figure out what is best for you and your children, or do you go on your knees seeking YHVH's will in everything.

Reflection:
* What are your answers to the questions posed in the second paragraph?
* Are you having a hard time handing over your life to YHVH?

Response:
Ask YHVH to help you to know Him more intimately. Make a concerted effort to build the love relationship with Him.

Running the race

Therefore, since we are surrounded by such a great cloud of witnesses, let us throw off everything that hinders and the sin that so easily entangles. And let us run with perseverance the race marked out for us.
Hebrews 12:1

We are running a race of faith—one in which we all need to "overcome" in order to finish. We have not overcome until we have persevered to the end. Overcoming is the victory of finishing. You are the best YHVH had to send to accomplish the purpose of your life. Only you can do and be what YHVH has sent you to do and be in this race. He is not even interested in you being the first to cross the line, or running with perfect form. He doesn't eliminate you when you fall. The only way you can lose this race is to step off the track and quit. No matter how far you've come, or how many times you have fallen, you can always get up and continue moving towards the finish line.

YHVH has a significant purpose for our lives that may not yet have been revealed. Who knows what multiplied results may come to the next generations because of your overcoming and finishing the course YHVH has set for you? These words, "Well done, good and faithful servant" awaits the overcomer. We are not in competition with one another. The race is not against others. Yeshua just wants us all to become what we were destined to be. We are here to finish the course as an overcomer.

Reflection:
* Over the past days has your relationship with YHVH deepened.
* Read Hebrews 12:1 again, are you committed to finishing your race and overcoming?

Response:
Write a prayer to Yeshua expressing your love and your desire to go ever deeper in your relationship with Him.

O Lord, thou hast searched me, and known me.
Thou knowest my downsitting and mine uprising,
thou understandest my thought afar off.
Thou compassest my path and my lying down,
and art acquainted with all my ways.
For there is not a word in my tongue, but, lo,
O Lord, thou knowest it altogether.
Thou hast beset me behind and before,
and laid thine hand upon me.
Such knowledge is too wonderful for me;
it is high, I cannot attain unto it.
Whither shall I go from thy spirit?
Or whither shall I flee from thy presence?
Psalm 139:1-7, 23-24 [KING JAMES VERSION]

Search me, O God, and know my heart:
try me, and know my thoughts:
And see if there be any wicked way in me,
and lead me in the way everlasting.
Psalm 139:1-7, 23-24

Examine your heart

Tremble and do not sin;
when you are on your beds,
search your hearts and be silent.
Psalm 4:4

My shield is God Most High,
who saves the upright in heart.
Psalm 7:10

Seeing into your heart

Vindicate me, Lord, for I have led a blameless life; I have trusted in the Lord and have not faltered. Test me, Lord, and try me, examine my heart and my mind; for I have always been mindful of your unfailing love and have lived in reliance on your faithfulness.
Psalm 26:1-3

You need to examine your heart and face up to its condition. The truth is that I thought I was doing fine, until Aldo wrote: "Mom, You are my gate keeper, but you have this... this... and this... sitting in your heart! How can you not see what you are doing to me and to yourself! How can your heart be so hard that you don't recognize the condition of your heart?" I realized that we are not always honest about what is going on in our hearts. The reason for this is that we are so full of pride and self-righteousness.

I was shocked that Aldo could see the real condition of my heart. As I prayed and opened up my heart to YHVH, I said, "Lord, it is so hard for me to know that my child knows all about my heart!" He answered, "Yes, I can see that your fear of man is greater than your fear of God." I was shocked because I know that you serve the one you fear. That day was a turning point in my life. How I thank YHVH that I was able to repent of the condition of my heart and start afresh, washed by the Blood of Yeshua. We should be more concerned about YHVH knowing the condition of our hearts than people.

Reflection:
- As Holy Spirit speaks to you, what is He showing you about the condition of your heart?
- Are you more interested in what people think of you than what the Lord does?

Response:
Write a prayer asking YHVH to help you to face up to the condition of your heart.

A heart of flesh instead of stone

I will give them an undivided heart and put a new spirit in them;
I will remove from them their heart of stone and give them a heart of flesh.
Ezekiel 11:19

YHVH replaced my stony heart with a new heart of flesh. As a result I have peace even in the midst of the challenges of a busy diary, being a mom, a friend and a wife. I truly believe that someone on their knees sees much further than they would standing on top of a hill. After spending so much time on my face before YHVH, I started to see a new thing; I began seeing a new life, and a new way, through my tears.

I understood what Yeshua meant about finding and losing your life (Matthew 10:39). This truth was central to Yeshua's teaching. He mentioned it six times in the four Gospels. To believe and obey this eternal fact is to live a life of abundance. But to ignore it is to accept the consequences of sin. Yeshua said: *The thief cometh not, but for to steal, and to kill, and to destroy: I am come that they might have life, and that they might have it more abundantly* (John 10:10 KING JAMES VERSION). Yet few people truly live a life of peace and ABUNDANCE in Christ. Abundance has to do with the condition of your heart; not your material possession or standing. He will give you a heart of flesh, and a life of abundance and peace.

Reflection:
- Have you come to the place where you have handed YHVH your heart of stone yet?
- If not what is holding you back from doing it?

Response:
Yeshua came to give you an abundant Life. Thank Him for this precious gift.

The fruit of our lives

The Lord saw how great the wickedness of the human race had become on the earth, and that every inclination of the thoughts of the human heart was only evil all the time.
Genesis 6:5

There is little revelation of the Kingdom of YHVH in the body of Christ. Yeshua is calling forth a remnant that will break through the Babylonian darkness and renounce their harlot DNA and lifestyles. He calls us to exchange our minds for the mind of Yeshua. This will become evident when we move our focus from seeking life and self-pleasure from other gods, to seeking Him and His will foremost in everything. YHVH wants us to have a pure love relationship with Him. Where we trust in Him placing all our faith in Him alone. Believing that nothing is impossible for Him, seeking first His Kingdom and His Righteousness. Then believing that everything else will follow.

For too long we have had a divided heart. The heart of a harlot. It is nothing other than an adulteress' heart. So one side of our heart produces good fruit, but the other side, the part that is not healed of all the wounds, is still affected by all the harlotry of Babylon. It is like two streams of water coming together. One is pure and one is full of dung (sin and iniquity). Like a woman holding her husband's hand on the one side, and her lover's on the other. That is how we live double lives. Loving Yeshua, but pleasing self and our own flesh with the world.

Reflection:
- Ask Holy Spirit to reveal the fruit of your heart to you?
- Then spend time in repentance asking Holy Spirit to cleanse your heart.

Response:
Write a prayer of recommitment to Yeshua.

Bride or Harlot?

You have to make a decision: To be His Bride or to continue in your old harlot ways imparted to you through your DNA? Are you living a double life with part of your soul loyal to Babylon and the other to the Kingdom of YHVH? Test the fruit of your thoughts and your behavior. Be honest with yourself and Holy Spirit. It is important that you do this so that the enemy has no legal right to touch you and your family. In the previous piece we asked Holy Spirit to reveal the state of our hearts to us. What did you do with what He revealed to you?

You have to choose to apply the Blood and renource the DNA of the harlot Baal and Jezebel that is in you. We have to rebuke the enemy in the name of Yeshua, renouncing our Babylonian lifestyles. Stop living according to your old ways! Ask Abba Father to fill your heart with His Kingdom life. *Create in me a pure heart, O God, and renew a steadfast spirit within me. My sacrifice, O God, is a broken spirit; a broken and contrite heart you, God, will not despise* (Psalm 51:10, 17). The world waits to see the children of YHVH manifest the fruit of Holy Spirit: Love, peace and power of the real Kingdom of YHVH.

Reflection:

* Continue allowing Holy Spirit to speak to you and reveal the true state of your heart.
* Read Psalm 51—King David's prayer of repentance. Make it personal and pray it to YHVH, trusting Him for grace and mercy.

Response:

Write a prayer asking Abba Father to fill your heart with His Kingdom Life.

Keep yourselves from idols

Little children (believers, dear ones), guard yourselves from idols—[false teachings, moral compromises, and anything that would take God's place in your heart].
1 John 5:21 [AMPLIFIED BIBLE]

The word Baal means master, lord or "husband." The harlot bride serves idols and is married to Baal. You will know that something is an idol in your life if you put up a big fight when it is taken away from you. Many of the things we fight over are the idols in our lives. We become angry when something we adore is taken from us or when we fear that it might be taken from us. These are all the things we cherish above being consecrated and set apart to YHVH.

We "burn incense" to the work of our hands and the imaginations of our minds when we take self-exalted pride in our accomplishments. Normal things such as the stock market, your business, job, money, your children, your body, diets, sports, and entertainment can all work together for our good. They become idolatrous when we put our trust and hope in them, rather than in Yeshua. By doing this we become our own gods. This was the lie Satan told to Eve in the Garden of Eden: If we could know what YHVH knows, we would become like Him. Do you realize that when you manipulate people, through the spirit of Jezebel in you, and have the attitude of "I will control them with my power and my tongue" that you are your own god?

Reflection:

- YHVH is speaking a stern word to us. What was your immediate response as you read these words?
- Did the things that you are holding onto too tightly spring to mind? What would your reaction be if they were all taken away from you?

Response:

Write down what Holy Spirit has revealed to you. Then spend time in prayer repenting. Re-commit yourself to Your Heavenly Bridegroom.

Freedom or a lie?

"...I have seen something horrible: They commit adultery and live a lie. They strengthen the hands of evildoers, so that not one of them turns from their wickedness. They are all like Sodom to me; the people of Jerusalem are like Gomorrah."
Jeremiah 23:14

Adultery, both spiritual and natural, is one of mankind's most hideous sins. People living in adultery live a perpetual lie. Generally the root is in your DNA. Aldo explains it like this through Wisdom: 'The rain of hell, from an unrepentant, iniquitous DNA falls on a broken heart and defiles it. Keeping it in bondage to prevent the person from becoming the pure Bride of Christ. No other sin brings so much destruction in life. Adultery in the spiritual realm will cost you the intimacy of a pure relationship with Yeshua. In the flesh it will keep you from intimacy with your spouse.

Spiritual adultery causes people to say: "I am not one with YHVH, I cannot hear His voice, and I feel distant from Him." This never goes unnoticed by Him. It is all because of a double heart. There is a sincere desire to love YHVH, but there is also a desire to accomplish something for yourself at the same time. All this is done under the banner of being Christian.' I look back at my life and I think what a fool I have been! It is only now that I have come to the place where I live in the heart of YHVH, in His peace, in His love, and in His will. And the fruit of this is freedom in Christ.

Reflection:

- The choice that we have to make is whether we will turn from our wicked ways or not.
- As you spend time in Holy Spirit's presence ask Him to shine His Light into your heart. What do you find there? And what are you going to do about it?

Response:

If you are feeling distant from YHVH examine your heart—if it is divided then make a choice and write about it below.

Facing the condition of our hearts

The eyes of the Lord are everywhere, keeping watch on the wicked and the good.
Proverbs 15:3

Christian growth means facing the condition of our hearts. I will share an example from my life. I thought I was fine until Aldo wrote to me: "Mom, you are my gate keeper, but you sit with this… this… and this… in your heart! How can you not see what you are doing to us! Your heart is so hard that you don't recognize its condition?" I realized that we are not even truthful with ourselves about what is in our hearts. We are so full of pride and self-righteousness. I was shocked that Aldo knew about the real condition of my heart. As I prayed and opened up my heart to YHVH, "Lord, It is so hard for me to know that my child knows all about my heart!" He answered, "Yes, I can see that your fear of man is greater than your fear of God." I was numb, because you serve the one you fear.

That day was a turning point in my life. I will never ever forget it. But, how I thank YHVH that I could repent of the condition of my heart and start afresh, washed by the Blood of Yeshua. Why is it that we are so concerned about people knowing what is going on in our hearts, but we don't care that YHVH sees it all?!

Reflection:
- Who do you fear and who are you serving?
- What does the condition of your heart look like today?

Response:
Tell Holy Spirit what you are going to do about it.

Walking in and with Holy Spirit

And My people, who are called by My Name, humble themselves, and pray and seek (crave, require as a necessity) My face and turn from their wicked ways, then I will hear [them] from heaven, and forgive their sin and heal their land.
2 Chronicles 7:14 [AMPLIFIED BIBLE]

No matter how religious or 'spiritual' we may think we are, unless we are walking with Holy Spirit we will not see the need for repentance and revival in our lives. Only then will the true state of our hearts will not be revealed to us. Sometimes we just need to stop and hear what Holy Spirit has to say about the condition of our hearts. When we do this our eyes will be opened, and if we truly love YHVH then we will be ready and eager to change direction.

Unless we walk in the Spirit YHVH cannot flow through us. Revival comes in our lives when we yield to Him, and when God's people are found walking in Holy Spirit. It is only here that you will find true repentance. It is when we reach this place that the fruits of our repentance will be visible for everyone to see. We don't need a new program to lead us into revival. No, true revival comes through the power of Holy Spirit and is sent down from on high by YHVH. We will experience genuine revival when we humbly allow Him to search our hearts, leading us to repent of our arrogant, hardened and loveless hearts—then Holy Spirit will take control of our lives and lead us step by step in His perfect will.

Reflection:
*   As you bow before YHVH open yourself to Him. Allow Holy Spirit to move in your heart. What is he showing you about the condition of your heart?
*   Are the fruits of repentance visible in your life?

Response:
Humble yourself before YHVH asking Him through Holy Spirit to take control of your life.

Serve Him in the world

And He said to them, "Go into all the world and preach the gospel to all creation."
Mark 16:15

Times of refreshing help prepare us for everyday life; they are not meant to separate us. I see a new trend in the body of Christ. People don't want to work, or study anymore. They want to stay at home "in the presence of the Lord." I really don't understand this, because to be in the presence of the Lord is a 24/7 lifestyle. Nowhere in the Word can I find that Yeshua said to stay at home. What I do see is Him sending out His disciples and instructing them: To preach the Gospel, establish His Kingdom here on earth, and serve others being His hands and feet in the world! He said we are to Go!

Why would I rather isolate myself from everything instead of going into the world? Every day we are confronted with challenges; when you study, when you are a mother at home, or a business person—you are confronted with the world. Yeshua uses all these tests to mirror and show us the true condition of our hearts. He uses these tests to humble us, to make us dependent on Him and Him alone. He wants us to overcome, because unless you overcome the world, you will not be called an overcomer—the Remnant of Christ. He transforms us into His likeness using our everyday situations.

Reflection:

* As you examine your heart what is preventing you from going out into the world and serving Yeshua?
* Do you see the Christian lifestyle as a 24/7 lifestyle?

Response:

Commit yourself to preaching the Gospel, serving others, and being Yeshua's hands and feet to those you meet.

Your heart, His garden

And he will be like a tree firmly planted [and fed] by streams of water, which yields its fruit in its season; its leaf does not wither; and in whatever he does, he prospers [and comes to maturity].

Psalm 1:3 [AMPLIFIED BIBLE]

The Believer's heart is Yeshua's garden. He bought it with His precious blood; then He enters it claiming it as His own. How many areas of your heart belong to Him, and how many belong to you right now? You have to get off the throne and allow Him to take control over every area of your life. Your garden is not open to everyone. It is enclosed so that the desires of your flesh and what is acceptable to the world will no longer be acceptable to you. People want to believe there is no harm in this or that. There is a consistent pull to draw us towards the world and its ways. I see how I have to fight to keep my heart closed to my flesh. That is the price that we must pay in order to have our hearts set apart for Yeshua.

Your garden is a place of beauty in Yeshusa's hands. His garden produces the best flowers, with the loveliest fragrance. This is as a result of the time and the pruning that went into cultivating each flower. I have seen that after the most painful pruning season the rarest and richest of white lilies and roses bloom in the place that Yeshua now calls His own—that which is no longer shared with   the world.

Reflection:

- Have you ever thought of your heart as a garden? Consider it now—what is growing in it?
- Who is in charge of the garden of your heart?

Response:

Write a prayer setting your heart apart for Yeshua.

Seek Him first

Your garden is a place of growth. With Him as the gardener, you will not stay undeveloped, but will always bear buds and blossoms. We grow in grace, in love and knowledge of YHVH. Your garden is a place of rest and peace. It is the place where Yeshua can manifest Himself. Often we worry and we are like Martha working so hard that we have no time for Christ. We should be like Mary whose only desire was to sit at His feet and receive the sweet showers of His love watering her garden daily.

People want a relationship of peace and love with YHVH where He controls their life? To have this you must take your hands-off, allowing Holy Spirit full control. Are you willing to do this? If not, are you willing to surrender everything to Him giving Him permission to move you out of the way and help you? Are you willing to die to self? If not, are you willing to give Him full permission to kill your fleshly desires and all of self? To humble yourself so that nothing will ever be more important than Yeshua? How badly do you want this love relationship? How desperate are you for this abundant Life that Yeshua died to give you? This my friend is Yeshua's dream for you—do you really want it?

Reflection:
* Are you someone who has wondered what it takes to have an ever deepening love relationship with YHVH?
* As you read this piece are you prepared to do what it takes?

Response:
Write a prayer of commitment.

Oneness with Yeshua

Who may ascend the mountain of the Lord? Who may stand in his holy place? The one who has clean hands and a pure heart, who does not trust in an idol or swear by a false god.
Psalm 24:3-4

Intimacy is a place of "oneness." Oneness asks that you give one hundred percent of yourself: Body, soul and spirit. The deepest part of who you are. You have to trust the other person with your heart. To trust that they will not trample on it. That they will treat it with respect making you feel safe and secure in their love. This is the kind of love that leads to "oneness", which in turn leads to complete intimacy!

When I submit myself to Christ I submit myself to becoming one with Him. He is Holy and wants me to live in "oneness" with Him. Every time I turn my back on holiness I can immediately feel how the distance between us grows. In "oneness" there is no distance. So how can I stay in "oneness" with Yeshua? I believe with all my heart in "Light and Truth" because that will bring true Life. Darkness is the source of death in your heart. The truth He is looking for is that I recognize the true condition of my heart, and the moment that I see it I sincerely repent for the first time. For such a long time I was deceived and I did not recognize the true condition of my heart. Those veils that hide our hearts' condition are called "denial." And denial will kill you!

Reflection:
* Are you hiding behind the veils of denial covering your heart?
* Come before Yeshua in sincere repentance.

Response:
Tell Holy Spirit how much you wish to know "oneness" with Yeshua.

Search me, O God!

Search me, O God, and know my heart; try me, and know my anxieties; and see if there is any wicked way in me, and lead me in the way everlasting.
Psalm 139:23-24 [NEW KING JAMES VERSION]

The enemies' strategy is that you never recognize the true condition of your heart. That is why he wants you to believe that "oneness" with Yeshua is impossible to achieve. Darkness lives in our souls along with fear, lies, pain, hate and so many other hidden sins. There are even generational curses that have been forced on us by other people. When the Glory Light of YHVH shines into our inner man our soul is enlightened by the Spirit of Truth. Then we can begin to see the true condition of our hearts. Truth leads us to repentance, and repentance leads us to holiness. Our heart is one with YHVH's heart. So when we seek "oneness" with Him our hidden darkness is revealed. Before that we are not really bothered by the condition of our heart. But as you become "one" with Him the more the reality of the condition of your heart becomes evident.

We have so many ways of hiding the darkness in our lives. It can be through money, status, ministry, being extroverted or alternatively introverted. People are so busy living up to a certain image as they try to impress the world. But what about what is going on inside of their hearts? Is it pride, stubbornness, vanity or denial? Why is it that we, as man, run from the true condition of our hearts?

Reflection:
* Are you still hiding the condition of your heart: If so is it because you don't recognize it or because of pride?
* Do you want oneness with Yeshua?

Response:
If you want oneness then pray the prayer of repentance in Psalm 139:23-24.

Holiness is the presence of YHVH

Your word is a lamp for my feet, a light on my path.
Psalm 119:105

When we go on our knees and worship the King of Glory we trade; our tears for joy, our fears for faith, our pain for healing and judgmental cursing for blessing. Let's go and take the Blood of Yeshua and bring it to the trading floors. The sins of man are blocking the blessings of YHVH! Let's start repenting with pure humility for the condition of our hearts, for our ignorance, denial and pride!

Holiness is not the absence of sin, but the presence of YHVH in our lives. In His presence we won't want to serve Satan and Yeshua. With His fire in us, it is not a case of sinning, or not sinning: No, it becomes a way of living because the fire of YHVH devours the desires of the flesh and self. It burns away the impurities until we are living for YHVH alone. Holiness is walking the journey of sanctification. The more we repent with a genuinely broken heart—not merely saying the words because we want to please someone, but being washed by the Blood of Yeshua through true repentance—the more we will start to live pure and blameless lives. And if this is too hard for you and does not come from a humble heart, you have to search who's character you have—your father Satan's, or your Abba Father's?

Reflection:
- Whose path are you following: YHVH or the powers of darkness?
- Holiness is walking the journey of sanctification.

Response:
Recommit yourself to walk the journey of sanctification, allowing YHVH's Light to guide your way.

Giving freely

...we want you to know about the grace that God has given the Macedonian churches. In the midst of a very severe trial, their overflowing joy and their extreme poverty welled up in rich generosity. For I testify that they gave as much as they were able, and even beyond their ability. Entirely on their own.

2 Corinthians 8:1b-3

Paul wrote to the Corinthians about the Macedonian church, and he said that they gave themselves to the Lord first and foremost. Having a ministry, I am so aware of people thinking, "Ministries only want my money." No! You see Yeshua is our Provider; yours and mine. He wants "ALL" of us, not only our money! If He has me and everything I own in His hands, then it won't be difficult for me to sow in love. What is the first thing that I have to give to Yeshua? Not my money, but myself.

Please, do not give your money to YHVH if you haven't given yourself. Money cannot buy a love relationship with Yeshua. Money cannot even buy true friendship here on earth. Yeshua doesn't want money from you to fix anything in your life. To sow is a Kingdom principle and not a way to buy your place into Heaven. He wants all of us so that we will be able to rest in Him, trust in Him and then obey Him when he asks of us to sow into His Kingdom. Then, out of us having given ourselves to the King—out of a place of understanding and grace—we will start to give without murmuring, knowing that we are doing the will of our Father. This will be all important to us.

Reflection:

*   As you examine your heart can you honestly say that all of you belongs to Yeshua.
*   If this is so, then are you open to being obedient to Him no matter what He asks of you?

Response:

Ask Holy Spirit to examine your heart and show you where you stand in these matters.

Where your treasure is...

For where your treasure is, there your heart will be also.
Matthew 6:21

One day Aldo came home from the gym where he was training, I came into his room and realized he had been on his knees for a long time. "What is wrong Aldo?" I asked him. "Nothing Mom, my friend is in need, and I am just praying to Yeshua about the amount I should give to him. I want to bless him with all he needs, but Holy Spirit is saying to me that I should always ask Him first, because He wants to lead me so that I can obey His voice. Mom, I have so much to be thankful for, and I know Yeshua will provide for all my needs. So, now I can give my friend what he needs."

Later when Tinus and I sat down for coffee we spoke about how once again we were amazed by Aldo's desire to obey Yeshua's voice. He does not worry about tomorrow! I know YHVH sees my heart, so I cannot lie. So many times I have wondered about Aldo's future, his income, where he will live? And then I see again that he does not worry at all. Why? Because he knows Yeshua. Are we obedient to Yeshua or to our fears? Your heart will be where your treasure is. "Lord, today, I give You everything of mine, even my money. Please take control."

Reflection:
* As you honestly examine your heart before Holy Spirit—where is your treasure?
* You need to have your treasure and your heart in the same place.

Response:
Allow Holy Spirit to lead you in a prayer of repentance and commitment to YHVH.

The cry of my heart

But those who hope in the Lord will renew their strength. They will soar on wings like eagles; they will run and not grow weary, they will walk and not be faint.
Isaiah 40:31

I hear the fish eagle cry out as it soars above the dam, and in turn my heart cries out to Abba Father: 'Your love is real. In Your love I can be myself. I can laugh, I can cry, I can ask for forgiveness—and You forgive me immediately. It is in the stillness of Your love that I find myself. I could never find myself in the crowd, in the competition of the world, or in the voices of perfection. It is in You and You alone that I find acceptance—a pure, undivided love. Give me Your heart dear Lord, a heart that is filled with passionate love. I want to start everything from a heart undivided with Your love—a love that is real. Your love Yeshua that caused You to lay down Your life for Your friends. I want a love that will give up EVERYHING to stay in Your heart—undivided, and surrendered to You.

Yeshua, please take my heart captive to Your love. Make my life Your own and let me hear Your voice as loud as I hear the cry of the eagle. You see in my heart dear Lord, a desire to belong to You and You alone. The cry of my heart is to have an undivided heart that is surrendered to the King.'

Reflection:
* Do you hear Yeshua calling your name today?
* Stop and take time to listen to what He is speaking into your heart.

Response:
Pour out your heart to Yeshua telling Him how much you love and need Him.

A place of rest

Therefore my heart is glad and my tongue rejoices; my body also will rest secure.
Psalm 16:9

YHVH spoke to me, 'Retah, inside your heart is a place of rest. Come into My rest. I am waiting for you. When things go wrong know that I am YHVH. I AM still on the throne. It is not about your comfort but dying to self. Surrender everything to me Retah! I AM sovereign over your circumstances. Seek My Kingdom and My Righteousness first and all the rest will follow. Humble yourself under My mighty hand. Rejoice in what I AM doing in your life, even though you do not understand all of it. I AM the Way, the Truth and the Life.

In Me you have everything you need, for now and for eternity. Don't let the desires of your flesh, the pain in your heart, the love that you lost, the fact that you are not perfectly healed yet, or the enemy's lies telling you that you need material things to be happy draw your focus away from Me. Your ultimate challenge is keeping your eyes fixed on Me, no matter how you feel, how it hurts, or what the world says. Make Me, the center of your thoughts. Then, you will be able to view your circumstances from My perspective. I AM busy transforming you into My likeness and it is a process of sanctification. It is a process of fire.'

Reflection:
- Have you found the place of rest inside your heart?
- YHVH has a special plan for your life, but you need to fully surrender your heart to Him.

Response:
Write a prayer of surrender to YHVH.

A faithful heart

Jesus said to him, "I am the way, the truth, and the life.
No one comes to the Father except through Me.
John 14:6 [NEW KING JAMES VERSION]

We have to choose to call out to Yeshua instead of "self" for help. Our hearts are naturally inclined to go their own way. We have been examining our hearts and asking Yeshua to shine His Glory Light into us. Without the true knowledge of Yeshua and union with Him, we rely on our own ability to move forward. In the process we become tired and we give up! A new heart goes along with a sound mind and the development of changed thought patterns.

In the spirit realm it is only Spiritual things that are solid. True love is solid, real forgiveness is solid, to bless someone is solid, to pray YHVH's will is solid. To care, to serve, to walk in Truth and Light are all solid. *Yet you do not know [the least thing] about what may happen in your life tomorrow. [What is secure in your life?] You are merely a vapor [like a puff of smoke or a wisp of steam from a cooking pot] that is visible for a little while and then vanishes [into thin air]* (James 4:14 AMPLIFIED BIBLE). Here the Word teaches us that everything material looks like it is made up of vapor and does not have eternal value. Do I have a heart that is following hard after God or am I chasing after vapors.

Reflection:
- What has Holy Spirit revealed to you about the condition of your heart over the past days?
- As you sit in His presence ask Him to help you to reach the place where you have a new heart.

Response:
Write a prayer to YHVH and Yeshua expressing what is in your heart right now.

Love YHVH

Know therefore that the Lord your God is God; he is the faithful God, keeping his covenant of love to a thousand generations of those who love him and keep his commandments.
Deuteronomy 7:9

I ask you today do you love Yeshua with all your heart, soul and strength and with everything in you—I mean everything. This means that your heart is yielded to the divine will of your Abba Father for your life. Willingly you surrender to the purification and refinement process in every area of your life—all from a place of love and not because you have to! *And thou shalt love the Lord thy God with all thine heart, and with all thy soul, and with all thy might* (Deuteronomy 6:5 KING JAMES VERSION].

The foundation of this truth is based on His abundant love for us and our love and appreciation for His great work of redemption in our lives. But, at this moment there is a great war raging in the hearts and souls of those who are being prepared to be used as vessels of honor to the King. This is the battle of Light versus darkness within man's soul. *But I see another law at work in me, waging war against the law of my mind and making me a prisoner of the law of sin at work within me. What a wretched man I am! Who will rescue me from this body that is subject to death? Thanks be to God, who delivers me through Jesus Christ our Lord!* (Romans 7:23-25).

Reflection:
* How much do you truly love YHVH?
* Do you surrender willingly to His work in your life?

Response:
Tell YHVH how much you love Him.

A double law at work

But I see another law at work in me, waging war against the law of my mind and making me a prisoner of the law of sin at work within me. What a wretched man I am! Who will rescue me from this body that is subject to death? Thanks be to God, who delivers me through Jesus Christ our Lord!

Romans 7:23-25

Darkness' hidden agenda in my soul is to bring the fruits of "death in the spirit" out in me. This means I will not be able to hear Yeshua's voice. I will not thirst for righteousness but, will seek the ranking of the world. I will run after the acceptance of man, live a double life and hide behind a mask of pretense. I will do everything out of brokenness and my treatment of other people will be out of this place—killing, stealing and destroying people's lives. I will bring in false fire wherever I go, I will lie, be full of pride and will always see what I can gain from others.

Sin living in our members was imparted with the fall of man in the Garden of Eden. We are therefore born out of a "double" DNA and seed—one of fallen man and one of Righteousness. The fallen DNA brings death to me (body, soul and spirit) and separates me from the strongest desire which is intimacy with Yeshua. Because of this "double" in me, I serve both fear and faith; and have both Light and darkness in my members. I have a double mind, a double heart, a double belief system, and a double calling. You will find that your personal strength is insufficient to win this war.

Reflection:

- Do you recognize the "double" at work in your life?
- Which is winning out right now: Light or darkness?

Response:

What are you going to do about it?

____

____

____

____

____

____

____

By My Spirit, says the Lord

So he said to me, "This is the word of the Lord to Zerubbabel:
'Not by might nor by power, but by my Spirit,' says the Lord Almighty.
Zechariah 4:6

You are not going to win this war with a set of rules. No, you will only overcome by the Blood of Yeshua and love for your King. The healing comes through true repentance and a heart opened up to Truth, because only the Truth will set us free! What a devastating thought when you realize through Holy Spirit that you have a double calling. You are called by darkness to bring death and destruction into people's lives. You are called to break up a family or to destroy a ministry. This double calling will work through your pain and generational inheritance until it is acknowledged and brought to the Light.

Not many people get to this place. The "double" will be quite obvious in your life, your family and your children. But, when you are operating in that "double" you always point a finger at other people. You are unaware of the darkness raging in you and its devastating effect on your life. This "double" in you will only be exposed if you truly have a yearning for Yeshua, calling out to Him: "I am struggling, please help me fight this inward fight. Please Yeshua shine your Glory Light into my body, soul, and spirit. Show me the "double" in me, show me the brokenness in me. I cannot wage this war alone."

Reflection:

- Are you still at the place where you are pointing fingers at other people?
- Or have you come to the place where you are crying out to YHVH for help?

Response:

YHYH is waiting to hear your prayer today.

The condition of your heart

My shield is God Most High, who saves the upright in heart.
Psalm 7:10

Only when you come to the place of yielding to the Messiah, with a broken heart, in true love will your spirit open up to His Truth! By coming out of denial through the help of Holy Spirit I can start taking responsibility for my actions, repent, bring my broken emotions to Him and trade my darkness for His Light. And so my healing will start transforming me into His image and likeness and I will be able to begin living an abundant life! James speaks about being double-minded (1:8). *That person should not expect to receive anything from the Lord* (1:7).

It was the best day of my life when Yeshua started showing me the real condition of my heart. Yes, it was a devastating picture, but I love Him so, so much and was so grateful that He allowed Aldo through Wisdom to write to me: "Mom, you are a gatekeeper in my life and all your "double" darkness that you hold onto through your pain, DNA and seed was passed on to me. This is what is hidden in you Mom, and I got all of it from you! The enemy fights me and wants to kill me because you opened the window and traded."

Reflection:
- Psalm 7 says God saves the upright in heart.
- What is the condition of your heart right now?

Response:
Come before YHVH in brokenness and repentance allowing Him to begin His restoration work in you.

Giving joy to the heart

The precepts of the Lord are right, giving joy to the heart.
The commands of the Lord are radiant, giving light to the eyes.
Psalm 19:8

Husbands pass their darkness on to their wives, wives their darkness on to their husbands, parents to their children and so the cycle continues. How can we say we love our children yet choose to stay in denial and in darkness? It was a turning point in my life when Aldo revealed to me how people impart darkness into each other through covenants and ties; sexual, emotional, friendship, spiritual and business. Chantelle is a gate to Aldo and Aldo to her. So, if she has hidden darkness in her it will fight him and try to keep him from his calling in Yeshua, and the same is true with him.

I know what I am talking about, because together we are walking out of brokenness and into wholeness. Before Aldo and Chantelle got married they had to deal with the darkness and brokenness inside of them. Abba faithfully allowed us to work through their pain in detail. Not easy, but a wonderful walk of humility—the price for freedom and healing! Together they take hands and work through it daily. I learnt so much from what Wisdom revealed about both of them and believe me, the enemy hates that! He just wants to keep the "double" in all of us. He wants to steal Yeshua's anointing of Truth and Light in us and keep the "double" hidden in us.

Reflection:
- You have to choose whether you will walk in Light or in darkness.
- What do you want to impart to your loved ones and those around you?

Response:
Verbalize and write your response to Yeshua.

Don't be double hearted

YHVH will not allow His bride to be a harlot double-hearted bride. We need to choose Life or death! Blessing or cursing, Light or darkness! We have no other choice than to completely break with darkness, with gossip, with hate and the jealousy in our lives. Pray for those who hate you. Aldo writes to me that hate and anger in people looks like a volcano that erupts with fiery lava. And this fiery lava of hatred, anger, jealousy, gossip etc. are Satan's secret weapons used to destroy the person you hate so much. You see the fight is in the spirit. These thoughts and emotions are like witchcraft and curses. In this hatred you operate out of Satan's "double calling" in your life to kill, steal and destroy people!!!!!

And only the love of YHVH can bring you to a place where you are willing to say "I will lay it all down—husbands for wives, wives for husbands and parents for children." What does it mean? I need to acknowledge the darkness and "double" within me, and I need to acknowledge that I live a double life. How would I know? Typically, I will struggle to hear His voice, I will not be living an Abundant Life in Christ and I will not have an intimate love relationship with Yeshua.

Reflection:

- What have you learnt about the condition of your heart as you have journeyed through this theme?
- What is YHVH calling you to do about it?

Response:

What will your response be to His calling?

*You who are my Comforter in sorrow,
my heart is faint within me.
Listen to the cry of my people from a land far away:
"Is the Lord not in Zion?
Is her King no longer there?"
Is there no balm in Gilead?
Is there no physician there?
Why then is there no healing for the wound of my people?*
Jeremiah 8:18-19a, 22

Receive your healing

But for you who revere My name,
the sun of righteousness will rise with healing in its rays.
And you will go out and frolic like well-fed calves.
Malachi 4:2

Heal me, Lord, and I will be healed;
save me and I will be saved, for you are the one I praise.
Jeremiah 17:14

Return to me

For thus says the Lord God, the Holy One of Israel: "In returning and rest you shall be saved; In quietness and confidence shall be your strength."
Isaiah 30:15 [NEW KING JAMES VERSION]

Return to Me, and I will return to you, says the Lord of hosts. Many people in the body of Christ are sick because of the enemy's plan to cause strong selfish needs or desires within individuals. He accomplishes his plan by preventing us from experiencing the real love of YHVH. He uses negative life experiences and deceiving spirits in you and those around you to blind you to Yeshua's unconditional love and power. The more you are blinded by Satan, the greater your desire for your own fleshly desires and selfish needs to be satisfied. Later, you convince yourself that only you can fulfill your needs. You blame everyone around you for your pain, rejection and unhappiness in your marriage.

The next step is masturbation, self-satisfaction, adultery, lusting with the eyes. You will become self-focused, self-centered and self-righteous. You will fight the truth of YHVH's Word so that you can stay in darkness and to enable you to believe that you are right. Selfish thoughts and actions lead to self-satisfying. Through this the enemy comes with spiritual mantels of shame, guilt and fear. And if you don't deal with them, the next step is self-defensiveness, pride, greed, lust and ultimately disobedience to Yeshua's voice. Once a disobedient lifestyle is established, the enemy brings inner turmoil and outer conflict thereby causing increased emotional wounds and spiritual deception.

Reflection:
* As you read these stern words what was your immediate reaction? This will give you a good indication of where you find yourself right now.
* YHVH says that "In returning and rest you shall be saved." Do you desire His healing in your life?

Response:
Express your heart and where you find yourself right now to Holy Spirit as you sit in His presence.

____

____

____

____

____

____

Kingdom of Light vs. kingdom of darkness

"I will give you the keys of the kingdom of heaven; whatever you bind on earth will be bound in heaven, and whatever you loose on earth will be loosed in heaven."
Matthew 16:19

Spiritual darkness, deception and dilution open the door for demonic influences and desires to enter your life. The results are negative behavior patterns such as aggression, lust, sexual dreams, pride, and the Jezebel spirit operating through you as you manipulate people to follow your beliefs. You will also experience withdrawal into fantasy worlds where you will be focused on self-satisfaction. These are all a part of the schemes that the enemy uses to try and keep us "from facing our pain." He causes us to run away from the truth and reality to satisfy all kinds of fleshly needs. All of these are ways of escaping and coping with your inner turmoil and stress.

We don't understand that whatever we do on earth connects with either the kingdom of darkness or the Kingdom of Light. Satan doesn't want you to leave the church; he only wants you to have mixed seed, live a double life, and believe that the only thing that counts is that Yeshua loves you. We are deceived into believing that we don't have to worry about deliberate sin. When this happens Satan has you in his claws. He needs people to stay in adultery, masturbation and lust producing seed for the Nephilim! The bride of Christ been blind all this time? Satan is raising up an army whose seed he can use!

Reflection:
* You cannot live in the Kingdom of Light and the kingdom of darkness at the same time. Which will you choose?
* Are you prepared to renounce this world in order to receive your healing and the keys of YHWH's Kingdom?

Response:
How are you going to respond to what you have read today?

____

____

____

____

____

____

____

Repentance the first step

Heal me, Lord, and I will be healed; save me and I will be saved, for you are the one I praise.
Jeremiah 17:14

As our souls are healed we become less fearful of what YHVH might expect of us. We grow in trust working towards complete confidence in God. All of this helps us to hear His voice. As we mature and heal we begin running the race of faith. How? By ridding ourselves of the "dung" as Aldo calls it (the unbelief, the doubt, the sinful thoughts, the anger, and the wrong beliefs) in our minds. The first step is to repent of the things that Holy Spirit has shown us. Then secondly, we must replace the evil thoughts with God's truths. Paul calls this "renewing the Spirit of our minds."

It is shocking how many people operate in New Age philosophy. This is all about the improvement of self; my will, my way and my desires, it is completely self-centered. Whereas Holy Spirit calls us to live a life where the emphasis isn't on us. As children of YHVH we live a Christ-centered life that is being transformed to the image of Christ. Day by day we take on His nature, character, attitudes, beliefs, likeness and His mind. Our new life does not try to improve the old self, no; the old self needs to die. Yeshua died to bring us healing and wholeness. He is the only One who can save us and heal us.

Reflection:

- Allow Holy Spirit to begin to identify the "dung" in your life. Open your mind, your heart and your spirit to Him.

Response:

What is He saying to you? Begin to journal His revelations as He leads you through this process of receiving your healing.

Confess your trespasses

Therefore confess your sins to each other and pray for each other so that you may be healed. The prayer of a righteous person is powerful and effective.
James 5:16

It was late at night, and I was alone in Cape Town. My family had returned home to Hartbeespoort Dam. After I dropped them off at the airport I returned to our beach house and I sat watching the waves. They were in perpetual motion—rolling in and out again, never stopping. It struck me that our sanctification process the same—it too never stops. The deeper you allow Holy Spirit to go, the more He will reveal to you. But you have to be willing for His Glory Light to shine into your heart and expose your pain.

Healing and sanctification do not automatically take place when we receive Yeshua as our Savior and Lord. However, the potential for healing and the process of healing begins at that point. I have seen that inner healing occur gradually over a period of time. The greatest keys for healing are unconditional love, acceptance, mercy, grace and forgiveness. Healing of the heart can only occur in an atmosphere of acceptance—one free from any form of condemnation. Appropriating the ministry of Yeshua, to heal the broken hearted, is one of the most powerful and effective experiences in preparing you to fully enter into the Kingdom of God. YHVH promises us in His Word that if we confess our sins He will forgive us and heal us.

Reflection:

* Have you begun to appropriate the healing that is yours in Yeshua.
* The greatest keys for healing are unconditional love, acceptance, mercy, grace and forgiveness. How are you appropriating the keys for healing in your life?

Response:

Write a letter to Yeshua sharing your heart with Him.

A healed heart

I will give you a new heart and put a new spirit in you;
I will remove from you your heart of stone and give you a heart of flesh.
Ezekiel 36:26

The more hurt, oppressed and misunderstood you feel, the easier it is to fall into self-pity. Breaking negative patterns and old thought processes is a battle. Identify them and ask Holy Spirit to help you create new patterns. Invite Him into your pain until it no longer exists. Ask Him to expose the lies that you believe to be real and to show you the truth because the truth will set you free! Yeshua moves when we pray. Self-pity is never satisfied, because it always demands more and more!

Abba, in Yeshua's Name we repent of our selfish hearts. I do not rejoice in every situation, as Your Word teaches me I should. I become stuck in self-pity. I complain and compare myself to others. I feel sorry for myself and it has kept me away from You. I haven't been able to see that any good could come from these trials I am going through. But today, I choose to trust You. Please help me to die in self, and to think of others instead of only about myself. Help me to break this evil cycle of self-pity and self-centeredness in my life. Mold me into Your image. Thank You for helping me to see that when I wallow in self-pity it is only me and my hardened heart that suffers. I love You Yeshua!

Reflection:
* As you prayed this prayer what did Holy Spirit reveal to you?
* Spend some time allowing Him to minister to you.

Response:
Then write down what He has said and your response to His words.

Press on toward the goal

I press on toward the goal to win the prize
for which God has called me heavenward in Christ Jesus.
Philippians 3:14

YHVH wants to heal our painful memories! But first we have to acknowledge and release them to Yeshua for healing. Holding on to past, and negative memories can hinder your future. Ask Yeshua to show you the lies that have become your reality and your truth. Then ask Him to replace these with His Truth. Attaining the Resurrection Life in Christ involves pressing on to the goal. Let's ask Holy Spirit to bring into our minds the hurting memories that need to be healed. Some memories may be obvious and others may be buried. Do not ignore any memory that Holy Spirit brings to your mind—consider it. Once you recognize a negative memory, pray....

Abba Father, in the name of Yeshua, I release to You for healing all the wounded, hurting, negative memories of my life. Please shine Your Glory light on these situations and the pain in my heart. Reveal Your Truth in my conscious and subconscious mind, from my conception through to my birth, the first years of my life, my childhood, my adult life up to this moment. I ask You to enter into these memories and to expose the lies and to bring the Truth so that I can be healed. Help me to deal with these and to forgive where I need to forgive and to accept that which I need to accept.

Reflection:
* Write down the memories that Holy Spirit brings to your remembrance.
* Then pray the prayer above over each memory.

Response:
Do whatever Holy Spirit tells you to do in relation to each memory.
Record it so that you can stand on the Truth that He reveals to you.

The Truth will set you free

To the Jews who had believed him,
Jesus said, "If you hold to my teaching, you are really my disciples.
Then you will know the truth, and the truth will set you free."
John 8:31-32

I see people I meet fight against the Truth—because of what is still inside of them. This is why Abba wants us to be free of the mixed seed. If you don't break free, you will not be able to tell right from wrong. When you start understanding how Baal operates, then you see Baal's character in all these fleshly arguments. People say: "But God told me it is all right to leave my husband;" or "it is all right to compromise;" or "it is all right to have an emotional friend because my wife is not there for me." Come on! Jesus' road is narrow, so stop compromising because it will catch up with you.

Jehovah is a righteous and Holy God, whose standards are far above ours. He is a God who loves His creation and offers to us the gift of Salvation. But, we must apply His Salvation to all the broken areas of our lives. Most of our pain and issues come from a wound. There is a lie at the heart of all of our wounds that seals it and keeps it in place. Ask Yeshua to switch on His Glory Light and shine it over your wounds. Ask Him to show you the lies, the judgments and the Truth. It is only the Truth that will set you free.

Reflection:

- Where are you compromising in your life?
- What is stopping you from being set free?

Response:

Sit in Abba Father's presence and as Holy Spirit speaks to you, allow Him to lead you in repentance.

God offers healing

Then your light will break forth like the dawn, and your healing
will quickly appear; then your righteousness will go before you,
and the glory of the Lord will be your rear guard.
Isaiah 58:8

God offers us healing, but Baal offers us the things of the world and of the flesh: The abuse, cruelty, manipulation, lust, greed, self-righteousness, strife, pride, jealousy and all the self-justifying we so easily get caught up in. These only further ensnare us into sinning against the one true God. If there is still anger and rage in your heart—you have to start by making the choice to forgive. If not, un-forgiveness will become the judgment that will allow your wound to become the door through which your pain is targeted.

Forgiving and releasing from the heart removes the root of bitterness from our hearts. BUT THE HEART MUST BE HEALED to prevent the bitterness from returning. YHVH wants to heal the pain, changing it into His perfect love. When I speak of your heart I speak of your inner man, your spirit (the part that relates to YHVH) and your soul, mind and emotions. Our painful experiences are locked into the permanent memory bank of our minds, whether conscious or subconscious. This affects our spirit and can even wound it. We live life according to our painful negative experiences and they can control our behavior. This stored pain and past generational DNA pain causes many people to be bound into negative thought and behavior patterns. For us to walk in freedom these patterns must change.

Reflection:
* What are the painful experiences that are preventing you from receiving God's healing in your life?
* Whom do you need to forgive today?

Response:
Make a list of the people that you need to forgive and bring them before Abba Father, speaking out forgiveness over each name.

Protected by YHVH

May the Lord answer you when you are in distress; may the name of the God of Jacob protect you. May he send you help from the sanctuary and grant you support from Zion. May he remember all your sacrifices and accept your burnt offerings.
Psalm 20:1-3

There are many occasions when people disappoint us. Sometimes we are discouraged by situations and even with ourselves. But we must never give up! Often issues are simply beyond our control and Yeshua is waiting for us to hand them over to Him. We allow ourselves to become so frustrated. I have seen that most of the pain in life is caused through unmet needs, unresolved issues and hurts that have not yet healed. These are the wounds in people's lives. When you don't invite the Glory Light of YHVH to expose the hurts they manifest and come out through your pain.

The Light exposes the lies that have caused our wounds, and the judgments that keep these lies in place. Most of all, though, the Light shows us the Truth. Because only the Truth can set us free. Yeshua is saying to me, "Retah, be on guard all the time, make sure your walls are built—because the enemy is out there sending the little foxes to destroy my children's land. Don't move My child—stand and be safeguarded with the armor of Light. The enemy hates that I reveal the truth in the hearts of My people. But I don't want My bride to be part of the Harlot bride. Stand My child I will protect you."

Reflection:
- Have you allowed people or situations to discourage you? Think about what you have read today.
- Where is the first place that you run to when you are distressed? Read Psalm 20:1-3 again.

Response:
What are you going to do about the answers to the questions you asked yourself in the Reflection? Pray verses 1 to 3 of Psalm 20 back to YHVH.

Do not open the door

The night [this present evil age] is almost gone and the day [of Christ's return] is almost here. So let us fling away the works of darkness and put on the [full] armor of light.
Romans 13:12 [AMPLIFIED BIBLE]

When people speak disappointment over you it is a deceiving little fox that sneaks in before you know it. The enemy's plan is to distract you from YHVH. He even bewitches YHVH's children with words and many of them cannot even see it. All too many of them believe everything they hear. Demons also speak, so we need to know Yeshua's voice. Those other voices just want to distract and disappoint you. The simplest irritation or unfulfilled expectation can then turn into a mountain of frustration. The enemy does all of this to open the door in your heart. Once that door is open he will weigh you down. He will rob you of your faith in Yeshua. He will take away your hope and all of your joy.

Look at yourself today. Have you opened the door? Or did you give all your frustrations and your questions to Yeshua? Take time to stop and take all your thoughts captive, communicate with Holy Spirit and He will lead you back into peace and healing. We, as the body, need to get to a place where we start living a mature life in Christ. You cannot forever look towards man for acceptance. So many people have pain from being rejected and I see it in all of our lives. This is because we are not rooted and grounded in Christ.

Reflection:
* Have you opened the door to the enemy?
* You have to make a choice about how you want to live.

Response:
What are you going to do about it?

The evidence of healing

But the fruit of the Spirit is love, joy, peace, forbearance, kindness, goodness, faithfulness, gentleness and self-control. Against such things there is no law.
Galatians 5:22-23

Why is "self' fulfilment so important to us? Could it be because we are not prepared to face the hurts, pain and rejection of the past and bring them to Yeshua? That in fact we cherish them? Why is it we would much rather escape and live in an imaginary world where we call the shots, where we are loved, where we indulge the cravings of our flesh? Instead of living in the here and now that Yeshua has blessed us with we are stuck in the past or we live a double life.

So many people in depression are being tormented by Satan with various torture tactics. When your children are on Ritalin, you can know that something is wrong inside their souls. Pray, that Holy Spirit will switch on His Glory Light so that we can start seeing the truth in our souls, the true condition of our hearts. Today, the Spirit of the Lord calls out for us to "show the house to the house." It is time to measure your heart and be honest about what is going on in your life. The true house of YHVH is measured by love, faith, mercy, grace, peace, life, rest, joy, hope, forgiveness, acceptance, righteousness, praise, worship, turning the other cheek, submitting to each other and having a passionate love relationship with Yeshua.

Reflection:
*   What did Holy Spirit say to you as you read this piece?
*   How are you going to respond to what He is saying?

Response:
Write your response to Holy Spirit's message to you.

More than a conqueror

Yet in all these things we are more than conquerors through Him who loved us.
Romans 8:37 [NEW KING JAMES VERSION]

Today, I want to say: "Thanks be to YHVH through Yeshua our King." We can be free and we can experience victory in this battle as we surrender to the will of YHVH for our lives. And I know that we will be "overcomers" or conquerors in Christ. To be an overcomer you have to overcome something. This might feel like a huge mountain that you feel is too high to even attempt climbing. But I have truly learned that the way to do it is step-by-step, day-by-day and second-by-second. I have learned to trust in Him alone. Most of the obstacles that we have to overcome are unresolved issues such as painful memories, hidden sin or the hidden painful emotions of anger and rejection.

Unresolved anger or pain leads to depression and infirmities and even confusion in people's lives. When unresolved issues or anger, known or unknown, reside in our hearts it causes us to listen through demonic filters. These filters distort our perceptions. Yeshua told me in love that nothing will just disappear: No! He said, "Ask My Glory Light to shine in those painful memories and allow Me to show you the lies that you believe, the judgements that are still in your heart and then allow Me to show you the Truth. Because only My Truth will set you free."

Reflection:
*   What are the things that are informing your perceptions? Are you listening through demonic filters?
*   Yeshua died so that you could be set free by His Truth.

Response:
Spend time praying Romans 8:37. Ask Holy Spirit to show you where you need to repent so that you can walk in Yeshua's Glory Light.

Facing painful memories

"I will give you the keys of the kingdom of heaven;
whatever you bind on earth will be bound in heaven,
and whatever you loose on earth will be loosed in heaven."
Matthew 16:19

Dealing with our painful memories is vital. Because of all the trauma that Aldo went through we have to go to every painful memory and deal with it. We do this step-by-step as Holy Spirit leads and guides us. I keep on praying day and night for Yeshua to reveal the Truth to his memories, to please shine His Light onto all of Aldo's hidden memories so that they are exposed. As I pray I bless him with a sound mind—the mind of Christ.

The awesome thing is that a blessing you speak over someone endures forever. Not like a curse that can be broken. There is so much power in blessing. As I bless and bless Aldo's hidden painful memories, the Light of Christ starts to shine on them and he begins to open up. Often we then discover and face the many lies and demonic structures around the memory. This is where a number of the infirmities hide. I know that this is where epilepsy hides. I also pray and intercede for the body of Christ, because it is not only Aldo who struggles like this, it is all of us! But, often we have so much pride that we do not want to face our pain and allow Holy Spirit to reveal and work with the hurt and lies.

Reflection:
* Are you too proud to allow Holy Spirit to reveal and work with the hurt and lies in your life?
* Consider Matthew 16:19 and what it means to bind in Heaven and loose on earth.

Response:
Spend time in prayer allowing Holy Spirit to speak to you and work in your life.

Climb the mountain step-by-step

Blessed is the one who perseveres under trial because,
having stood the test, that person will receive the crown of life
that the Lord has promised to those who love him.
James 1:12

We have a mountain in Hartbeespoort were we stay. Some time ago we decided to climb it: Tinus, Aldo, his friend Andre and I. I walked behind them and realized that Aldo couldn't do it by himself yet. But in front of him was Andre, his friend and personal trainer. Aldo had to hold onto him all the time, and behind him was his dad—who also didn't let go of him for a second.

As I looked at the picture I heard Holy Spirit say to me, "That's how you conquer a mountain step-by-step. I will be in front, and behind you, leading and guiding your every step." The Lord of angel armies protects us on all sides, never letting go. Aldo fell several times, or slipped on a rock, but they held on tightly that he always felt safe and secure. At the top he sat down and prayed, "Abba, how I thank You that I know I can do all things through You who strengthens me." It was a humbling moment, in spite of the difficulty. We looked over the dam and could see for miles. We did not even look at the rocks or steep climb. No, we rejoiced in the beauty that we saw—a much bigger picture than the difficulty of the climb.

Reflection:
*   What is the mountain you are facing at the moment? How are you tackling it?
*   Are you prepared to ask for help or are you trying to do it all alone?

Response:
Ask Holy Spirit to help you to deal with your pride and stubbornness.

You are a Faithful God

Your mercy, O Lord, is in the heavens; Your faithfulness reaches to the clouds.
Psalm 36:5 [NEW KING JAMES VERSION]

We all know that broken fathers break their children, and broken children become broken fathers. Brokenness causes such an evil cycle. But it becomes worse, because we start operating out of an "orphan spirit." Many years ago Aldo said to me, "Mom, I see an 'orphan spirit' in you." I thought, "well, maybe it is because I was in a hostel from grade one?" I had no idea what it meant to have an orphan spirit. But the longer I have walked the journey, the more I have come to realize what the depth of this condition means.

I came from a home where love was earned through works. Because my dad was broken himself, he did not know how to love "unconditionally." The children living under a system like this are hurt because they feel that they are never good enough. Feelings, emotions, pain and thought patterns are developed; the hurt and the pain quench the human spirit, resulting in an orphan spirit. I am not talking about a demonic spirit. It is our own spirit that causes us to feel alone, not good enough, insecure, that we do not belong and that we have to try to earn love. What an evil cycle. Spiritual orphans struggle to receive the Father's love, or even the love of people—all because of past hurt and rejection.

Reflection:
* Spend some time allowing Holy Spirit to reveal to you whether you have an "orphan spirit."
* Then allow Yeshua's love to wash over you as you bring your hurts and rejection before Him.

Response:
Read Psalm 36:5 again. Worship YHVH who is faithful and loves you unconditionally. Thank Him for His faithfulness to you.

Heal me, and I will be healed

O Lord my God, I cried out to You, And You healed me.
Psalm 30:2 [NEW KING JAMES VERSION]

You can know about the Father's love, but be unable to experience it. Even if you are in ministry—this could be you. An orphan spirit hides behind independence and the denial of pain, masking the true condition of the heart. Denial nearly killed me and is from the pit of hell. It covers you in thick layers that blind you to the truth. Orphan spirits control relationships through anger. They find their comfort and identity in achievements, position, and addictions. Out of their insecurity they need to be the best, to win at all costs, and to fit in no matter what it takes. They will walk over other people to get what they want. They are jealous, trying to earn the love of YHVH and people. Orphan spirits are rebellious seeking importance by "marrying well," physical appearance and activities. They do not trust man or Yeshua.

An orphan spirit cannot be driven out. The person's heart needs healing. We all need the unconditional love of Yeshua—only His love brings healing. Once we are healed by the love of our Abba Father we can begin the process of entering into mature sonship. And the world is crying out for the manifestation of the sons of YHVH. *For [even the whole] creation [all nature] waits eagerly for the children of God to be revealed.* (Romans 8:19 AMPLIFIED BIBLE).

Reflection:
* Allow Holy Spirit to speak into the depths of your heart right now.
* Don't carry the pain around any longer.

Response:
Come before Yeshua and allow Him to heal your pain so that you can walk tall as a child of YHVH.

Rejoice in your healing

Rejoice in the Lord always. I will say it again: Rejoice! Let your gentleness be evident to all. The Lord is near. Do not be anxious about anything, but in every situation, by prayer and petition, with thanksgiving, present your requests to God...
Philippians 4:4-6

I know that Yeshua wants our hearts healed because someone with an orphan heart cannot forgive, cannot receive love, cannot love and cannot trust. This is exactly what the enemy wants because you will struggle to walk in faith. The more healing I receive the more I am able to walk in son-ship. We must die to any and all ungodly beliefs that keep us from becoming sons of YHVH. Abba is waiting to decree our son-ship not only to the world, but to all the powers and principalities of hell. It is time to start operating in victory and to fight from a place of victory. It is time to ask forgiveness through the Blood of Yeshua and allow Holy Spirit to have full rule and reign in our lives so that we can be free and healed.

My healing started the day I humbly surrendered all of myself to Yeshua—withholding nothing. I chose to die to all that I was holding on to. It was so painful but, this was the best thing I could have done for myself and all those around me. Today, I just walk as a son of YHVH, rejoicing in His faithfulness. On good days and on bad days I choose to rejoice. Not, because of what I gain from it, but because of who He is.

Reflection:

*   If you have not begun to receive your healing then come to YHVH today and ask Him to touch your life.
*   Begin rejoicing in your healing.

Response:

Write a prayer of rejoicing to Abba Father thanking Him for His goodness to you.

____

____

____

____

____

____

____

____

____

____

Nothing is too hard for YHVH

My life is a walk of faith obeying Abba. Sometimes the world and even Christians mock me. But, I know my Abba and I am only interested in being faithful to His call, because I love Him, not so that He will heal my child through my works. Aldo received his healing through Yeshua's blood and by faith in Yeshua—nothing else!

Eight years ago YHVH told me to write *"a Message from God."* A true life story of a mom who cried out to God when her son was dying. She was so lost because of her orphan spirit and hardened heart. She had an encounter with the Most High God—El Shaddai—the Super-natural God who can do anything! The God for whom nothing is impossible. All you need to do is give your whole life to Him and trust in Him. Her son met Yeshua in Heaven and came back with a message from God, "I am on my way, but my bride is not ready...." Many letters followed from Yeshua's heart through a broken boy. Every time his mom looked at him, her heart broke over and over again. Until one day the boy asked her, "Will you please look at me through Yeshua's eyes? You are looking at me through your own brokenness, and you fail to see the goodness of YHVH."

Reflection:
- Is there a situation in your life that only YHVH can heal?
- Ask Him to show you the true motive of your heart for serving Him.

Response:
Write a prayer to YHVH expressing your love and trust in Him.

Trust and obey

Trust in the Lord with all your heart and lean not on your own understanding;
in all your ways submit to him, and he will make your paths straight.
Proverbs 3:5-6

Yeshua asked me to trust Him; and I continue to treasure this faith I have in Him. Faith on the one hand and hope in the other hand. When I finished the book it was time to find a publisher. One sent me a letter telling me we were evil. I still remember how I cried that night saying, "Dear Lord if Aldo's letters are evil, and if I am evil and fail to see it, please speak to me. I need You tonight! Please speak to me before I take this book to the printers." I fell asleep on a wet pillow.

I awoke with His Glory covering our bed. "Yeshua, is this You?" "Yes, it is Me." I forgot about the book, "Why are You so good to me?" "Because you love Me. Give Me the book." I gave Him the book and He blew His Spirit into it saying, "Everyone who reads this book will experience My Spirit, and it will be a best seller." I awoke knowing that I had met with Yeshua. I slept peacefully after that. The next morning Aldo wrote, "I saw Jesus was with you last night." Well, you can imagine the joy in my heart. It helped me to keep standing on His Word through the many instances when people made negative comments about the book.

Reflection:
- Do you allow people to influence your obedience and faith in YHVH?
- Read Proverbs 3:5-6 again and allow Holy Spirit to speak to you.

Response:
Speak to YHVH telling Him that you choose to trust Him and not man with all of your heart.

Sin of the parents

'The Lord is slow to anger, abounding in love and forgiving sin and rebellion. Yet he does not leave the guilty unpunished; he punishes the children for the sin of the parents to the third and fourth generation.'

Numbers 14:18

As you know I have a chat box day once a month and people phone in from all over the world. As I listen to them I hear their pain, I hear the cry of each heart. I have the answers for them there is so much that I could explain to them, but it is so difficult over the telephone—such a long distance separating us but I know Holy Spirit is in each one and He will lead. "Retah, my father-in-law died and now my husband is behaving exactly like him. I cannot stand it anymore. It feels like I am married to my father-in-law. My husband has the same anger, the same manners, the same words—I don't understand it. We fight so much I want a divorce!"

What is being experienced here is called ancestral (generational) dissociation from a broken person. The familiar spirits come into that broken part of the mind. There is a DNA memory of that person. When an ancestor's soul is fragmented, that broken part can be transferred or transmitted spiritually into a relative after death. It works exactly the same way as sin and curses that can be transmitted to future generations. So, why are we surprised that the broken, unsorted, unrepentant part of a person's soul can be transferred to other people in the bloodline?

Reflection:
- Spend some time in Holy Spirit's presence allowing Him to show you where you or someone close to you may have become open to receiving from a dead relative.
- Holy Spirit will lead you into all Truth if you will open yourself to Him.

Response:
Journal about what Holy Spirit has shown you and bring it before YHVH, bringing it under the blood of Yeshua.

YHVH heals DNA

May God himself, the God of peace, sanctify you through and through. May your whole spirit, soul and body be kept blameless at the coming of our Lord Jesus Christ.
1 Thessalonians 5:23

Yeshua told me nine years ago, "Retah, you will never preach what you haven't tasted." Well, about two years ago we went to hell and back in spiritual warfare. We only had Holy Spirit because nobody could help me or understand what we were fighting. It was a life and death fight for Aldo. And I know that (the broken part of someone who had died) was after his calling. A person who is broken in this way will come in and try to destroy your life and your calling. Just as you inherit features such as eye and hair color from your parents, so you can also inherit their disorders. As we went through the experience Holy Spirit faithfully led me through Wisdom. Aldo explained everything to us about inheriting the broken part of a person in your DNA.

We realized that just as traits are transmitted through genes, pieces of an ancestor's broken soul (mind and emotions) can be transmitted through the family bloodline. All this is in my book, *Save my DNA*. We experienced this first hand, and it was the most difficult time of my whole life, not even the accident was as difficult. The reason being that I didn't understand what was happening. I couldn't tell anyone about it and only after we overcame the situation was I able to write about it.

Reflection:
* Continue allowing Holy Spirit to minister and speak to you.
* If you need further help in understanding what is happening then read *Save my DNA*.

Response:
You can know that Holy Spirit will faithfully lead you—so spend time thanking Him for His care of you.

Set the captives free

The Spirit of the Sovereign Lord is on me, because the Lord has anointed me to proclaim good news to the poor. He has sent me to bind up the brokenhearted, to proclaim freedom for the captives and release from darkness for the prisoners.

Isaiah 61:1

The spirit is spiritual (John 3:6) and when we die those who know Christ as their Lord and Savior enter eternity. However the broken soul can be transmitted to future generations in the same way as curses and sicknesses. Our spirit is one with Holy Spirit and therefore cannot be touched by Satan or his demons.

The good news is that Yeshua paid the full price and we can minister to those broken parts. The legal right that the DNA has must be removed. We must repent of our DNA and stand in the gap. The ancient memory, as Aldo calls it, is in the mind (the soul) and is the old broken part filled with trauma, and unrepented hidden s n. It is inherited from an ancestor such as a grandfather or a mother. There will always be a legal right within DNA that has not been broken or repented of. Many times when people pray the DNA prayer and they do not know about this, there will be havoc. This is because that part loses its rights to stay, and they need to be helped to go into eternity. If not they stay! So make sure you find out what right it is holding onto—the spiritual generational DNA right. This is why Yeshua said I came to set the captive free and heal the broken hearted.

Reflection:
- As YHVH's child you have a right to Yeshua's healing.
- Make sure that you stand in the gap and claim your healing.

Response:
Thank Yeshua for His healing power in your life.

Healing Life

Whoever tries to keep their life will lose it,
and whoever loses their life will preserve it.
Luke 17:33

There is no growth in self-centeredness; it is not the way to healing Life in Yeshua. It only causes you to circle the mountain again and again. Self-centeredness is the source of sin, iniquity and darkness. It is all about you. In order to train properly so that you can run the race effectively you need to start looking at the bigger picture. You need to see that everything is not about you. You are just part of YHVH's Kingdom plan. And even if things are difficult and you are in the fire, you still hold on to your hope and your faith in Yeshua. Your faith and hope are not centered around your situation, but on your God who is so much greater than the situation. That is why we can never give up!

We struggle sometimes to abide in peace, because of our brokenness. Here in brokenness our "parts" or emotions that are not whole, are in darkness, in depression, in death, in sickness, in bondage or in shackles. Our fleshly deeds will not lead to wholeness and healing. All of us, every part, and every emotion need to be in right standing with YHVH— one with Him. It is out of this place of right standing with YHVH that we will find our rest and healing.

Reflection:
- If you want to receive your healing then you need to die to self.
- Have you been making everything about yourself? If so then it is time to stop.

Response:
Tell Abba Father that you are prepared to die to self.
That above all you want His peace and healing in your life.

Heal me, Lord

Heal me, Lord, and I will be healed;
save me and I will be saved, for you are the one I praise.
Jeremiah 17:14

When you die to self, you start to realize that you are born as a spiritual being. And as your spirit connects to Yeshua's Spirit you become one with Him. With every step along your spiritual journey you realize that material things are beginning to lose their value. You see how you have spent your entire life collecting riches for yourself. But, all of this is made up of temporal substance and will soon pass away like mist. As you continue, you realize that that which is visible in the spiritual realm are not your possessions that moth and rust can damage, but only your spiritual condition.

It was such a shock to me when Aldo started to write about this even before he could speak. All he saw when he looked at people was what was going on in their spirits. This has not changed; he still writes about the light or darkness that he sees in our spirits. Through his writings Holy Spirit has taught us about peoples' brokenness. He never sees or writes about the physical or the flesh. The focus is always on the spirit. The condition of the heart, is it sick or healthy? I have come to understand that we are so blinded by the world that we cannot see who we really are in Christ and what our purpose is.

Reflection:
- As you take a further step on your journey, stop and ask Holy Spirit to help you to see the condition of your soul.
- Are you sick or healthy? Whatever condition you are in Yeshua can heal you.

Response:
Come before YHVH and ask Him to heal your body, soul and spirit today.

Spirit of Truth in you

The Spirit of truth. The world cannot accept him, because it neither sees him nor knows him. But you know him, for he lives with you and will be in you.
John 14:17

The moment you absorb the Truth of YHVH into your inner being instead of having an intellectual knowledge of it you will be transformed. His Truth sets you free and enables you to live in His Light and Life. As you travel on your journey seeking His will, His Light, and His Life, your darkness will begin disappearing and you will begin to receive your healing. But, people are not always willing to deal with their pain and darkness.

Hear me, the darkness is starting to cover the earth. You need to be in the Light of Christ! You can no longer afford to live a double life. People think that no one knows what they are doing in their inner world, but Christ knows everything. It is the broken "parts," the emotions in people's lives that are an enemy to the people around them and to themselves. These broken parts break up families and destroy lives as far as they go, because they act out of pain. This is because they are in darkness, filled with lies, and judgments in their hearts. Broken people break other people. The inner thoughts and inner life of man is so real and visible in the spiritual realm, just as a heart and life filled with Truth and Light is. Allow the Spirit of Truth to heal your broken life.

Reflection:

- John 14:17 says ...*The world cannot accept him, because it neither sees him nor knows him. But you know him, for he lives with you and will be in you.*
- Do you know Him, and are you allowing Him to heal your broken places?

Response:

Write a prayer to YHVH telling Him where you are on your journey and asking Him to continue to heal you.

*For though we walk (live) in the flesh,
we are not carrying on our warfare according to
the flesh and using mere human weapons.
For the weapons of our warfare
are not physical [weapons of flesh and blood],
but they are mighty before God
for the overthrow and destruction of strongholds,
[Inasmuch as we] refute arguments and theories and
reasonings and every proud and lofty thing
that sets itself up against the [true] knowledge of God;
and we lead every thought and purpose
away captive into the obedience of Christ
(the Messiah, the Anointed One).*
2 Corinthians 10:3-5 [AMPLIFIED BIBLE CLASSIC EDITION]

Spiritual warfare— Fight the battle

Pulling down strongholds

For though we live in the world, we do not wage war as the world does. The weapons we fight with are not the weapons of the world.
2 Corinthians 10:3-4

Paul clearly tells us in verse four that we *…have divine power to demolish strongholds.* He instructs us to pull down the strongholds. He says we must *…demolish arguments and every pretension that sets itself up against the knowledge of God, and we take captive every thought to make it obedient to Christ* (v5).

We are to cast down imaginations and bring every thought into captivity. We are to use our spiritual weapons to come against every high thing that exalts itself against the knowledge of God—and so we learn that our minds are a battle field. We need to start training ourselves and our children to take up God's weapons and fight the fight. We must use the weapons that we have been given against anything that tries to keep our thought patterns and habits locked into the old way of doing things. We do not wage war as the world does. Do you know that fear, worry, hatred, bitterness, anger, shame, and control—need to be dealt with in your life and the lives of your family? You need to discover what the root cause is. Then you need to repent of it, and cast down the stronghold. Once you have done this replace it with the mind of Christ. This can only be done through prayer, repentance and applying the blood of the Lamb.

Reflection:
- As you read the Scripture what did Holy Spirit say to you?
- Ask Him to begin revealing where you have allowed strongholds to take root in your life.

Response:
Come before YHWH and ask Him to help you to wage war against the enemy.

The fig tree has budded – Part 1

He told them this parable: "Look at the fig tree and all the trees. When they sprout leaves,
you can see for yourselves and know that summer is near."
Luke 21:29-30

Today we are living as in the days of Noah. Daniel speaks of a dark cloud that will cover the earth. This cloud tells of a storm that we all know is coming. The end times are like this "storm." The only problem is that the body of Christ doesn't realize that we are in the storm. Already, we can feel its effect even though it has not yet arrived in full. There are many signs of the Lord's second coming, just as there were for His first coming. And Yeshua rebuked the leaders of His day for not being aware of the signs of His first coming that were evident.

Paul in his letter to the Thessalonians wrote that Believers could and should know the times and the seasons of the Lord's (second) coming since they were not deceived by darkness like the others. In 1 Thessalonians 5:1-6 we read about these signs. Below are the first three signs:
Now, brothers and sisters, about times and dates we do not need to write to you, (v1).
for you know very well that the day of the Lord will come like a thief in the night (v2).
While people are saying, "Peace and safety," destruction will come on them suddenly,
as labor pains on a pregnant woman, and they will not escape (v3).

Reflection:
* Are you aware that the dark clouds are gathering and the storm is fast approaching?
* Where are you placing your hope and trust—in the world and its systems or in Yeshua?

Response:
Express your thoughts and feelings to Holy Spirit.

The fig tree has budded – Part 2

Then He told them a parable: "Look at the fig tree and all the trees; as soon as they put out leaves, you see it and know for yourselves that summer is near.
Luke 21:29-30 [AMPLIFIED BIBLE]

P aul continues to talk to us about the signs of the End Times in 1 Thessalonians 5:4-6: *But you, brothers and sisters, are not in darkness so that this day should surprise you like a thief (v4).*
You are all children of the light and children of the day. We do not belong to the night or to the darkness (v5).
So then, let us not be like others, who are asleep, but let us be awake and sober (v6).

Yeshua links all of the events mentioned in 1 Thessalonians chapter 5 with birth pains. In Mathew 24:8 he says, *But all these things are merely the beginning of birth pangs [of the intolerable anguish and the time of unprecedented trouble]* [AMP BIBLE]. So if we consider today's events in terms of giving birth, we might say that prophetically all that is left is to push the baby out. The disciples asked in the same way that people today do, "So what will be the signs?" We, as the children of YHVH, need to know about the events happening that tell us that the labor pains are increasing in intensity. Yeshua tells us: *"Be always on the watch, and pray that you may be able to escape all that is about to happen, and that you may be able to stand before the Son of Man"* (Luke 21:36).

Reflection:

* Have you allowed yourself to be lulled into a sense of false security?
* Or are you fearful about what lies ahead?

Response:

Neither of the above are the reactions that YHVH's children should be having.
Spend some time writing down the correct things you should be doing as you await Yeshua's return.

Avoiding the corruptible seed

"Watch and pray so that you will not fall into temptation.
The spirit is willing, but the flesh is weak."
Mark 14:38

Douglas Hamp states in his book *Corrupting the Image* (www.douglashamp.com) "Based on the extensive investigation of many researchers, among them John Mack from Harvard, who interviewed on numerous occasions over one hundred abductees, we see the demons have been harvesting eggs from woman and sperm from men for many years." According to the testimony of some abductees, they are using the genetic material to create hybrid babies—this is a mix between themselves and humans—mixed seed. Their aim is to create an "alien" human hybrid (even though they don't look alien anymore—because they are living among us. So we have come full circle—just as in the days of Noah (Genesis chapter 6).

People live double lives thinking no one knows what is happening "behind the scenes" in their lives. As you are reading this people are having sexual dreams, (spiritual husbands and wives) and masturbating on a regular basis. They think no one knows—but they don't understand that the enemy has an end time plan using the children of YHVH to breed Nephelim babies. The demons are mingling their seed with the seed of men, just like the book of Daniel prophesied. You would not even realize what you are doing—this is how blind we are as the Harlot bride! Judgement is quickly approaching because of what we do in secret behind the scenes.

Reflection:

*   Where do you find yourself as you read this? What is Holy Spirit speaking into your life right now?
*   What do you choose today: To go deeper with your King or follow Satan?

Response:

Write your response below.

Beware the corruptible seed

The power of the horses was in their mouths and in their tails; for their tails were like snakes, having heads with which they inflict injury. The rest of mankind who were not killed by these plagues still did not repent of the work of their hands; they did not stop worshiping demons, and idols of gold, silver, bronze, stone and wood—idols that cannot see or hear or walk.

Revelation 9:19-20

Aldo wrote: *The new, humble Samuel saw that humble people stood on the sea of glass. They are shining like translucent glass. Samuel asked Wisdom: "Why can I see through them?"* Wisdom answered and said that it is because they are humble servants of God. The triune God is Father, Son and Holy Spirit. As children of YHVH we will not be able to have mixed seed in us, because all the plagues will fall upon us. Revelation 9:18 says: *A third of mankind was killed by the three plagues of fire, smoke and sulfur that came out of their mouths.* The rest of humanity who are not killed by these plagues will still not repent of worshiping the works of their own hands. They do not cease paying homage to the demons and idols of gold, silver, bronze, stone and wood that cannot see, hear or move.

In our lives we are continually fighting a mixed seed. I can see, more than ever before, how the enemy has blinded our eyes while he pursues his goal of making sure that we continue to live in Babylon. Right before our eyes we are watching as things unfold in Abba's grace. Wisdom reveals and explains through Aldo, then we see and experience them. We are in a time of Spiritual warfare like never before.

Reflection:
- We see the work of the enemy around us, but YHVH is so much stronger. How do you see His hand at this time?
- What is going on in your heart and life at the moment? What sort of seed is in your life?

Response:
Write down your thoughts and what Holy Spirit is saying to you about what you have read.

The fight within the DNA

Those who live according to the flesh have their minds set on what the flesh desires; but those who live in accordance with the Spirit have their minds set on what the Spirit desires.
Romans 8:5

People ask me, "Are you talking about flesh or spirit Retah?" Adam and Eve were covered in the Glory of God making them "transparent"—then sin came and they became flesh—"dark." But YHVH made a plan so that the sons of men would not need to die in self, the flesh; not only their spirits but also their souls will be saturated with Holy Spirit. Yeshua will live in their souls—that is the sanctification process—once again becoming transparent according to His image and likeness.

Yeshua's character will become your character, you will see what He sees, love what He loves and hate what He hates. You will be so sensitive to the things of the spirit. For years Aldo was saying that the fight is taking place in our DNA. At first I could not understand what he meant. But in our personal journey we have had to fight the DNA. All DNA has memory, therefore it holds the good, the bad, and the ugly. DNA also has senses and all of them need to be sanctified. Every day, Aldo tells us about the fight within the DNA. It is the satanic evil genetic, and superimposed DNA manipulations that create all the sickness and torment in people's lives. (If you missed this teaching you can listen to the mp3 recording: *Save my DNA*, on my website.)

Reflection:
- Who is winning the fight within your DNA – the flesh or the Spirit?
- What are you doing to make sure that your mind is set on what the Spirit desires?

Response:
Write a prayer asking Holy Spirit to help you express your desires to Yeshua to walk in His Glory Light.

Whose bride are you?

Let us rejoice and be glad and give him glory! For the wedding of the Lamb has come, and his bride has made herself ready.

Revelation 19:7

We have to wage warfare because while we are on earth we are in Satan's domain. We fight the unseen battle between good and evil. Most people in church have a hard time understanding that battle exists, even though they are not living the Abundant Life. They are influenced and bewitched by a satanic mindset. It is still all about "self"; their own happiness and pleasures here on earth.

Satan has successfully spun a foggy web that blinds them so that they are unable to see the Truth. This web's name is SELF, filled with New Age belief systems. It operates even in churches—causing people to seek their own happiness. It's all about my children, my life—it is all about me, me, and me. This is idolatry. You know that you are entangled in this web if these are still part of your life: False teachings; seeking events rather than the One True God; and people pleasing—being more worried about what people will say and their opinion of me than what Yeshua will say. This dark web is far from the Light of Yeshua where we live in transparency, acknowledging our struggles and simply being honest in love. We, as God's children, are in training for the end time battle. We are called to be the warrior bride—pure and selfless.

Reflection:

- Read John 10:10—are you enjoying Abundant Life in Yeshua?
- Whose bride are you?

Response:

Write down your thoughts and the things Holy Spirit has shown you today?

Fight between two kingdoms

For our struggle is not against flesh and blood, but against the rulers, against the authorities, against the powers of this dark world and against the spiritual forces of evil in the heavenly realms.

Ephesians 6:12

Satan copies everything and he is also preparing himself a warrior bride—a harlot bride. That is why the evil seed must be removed from our lives. Our seed must be sanctified. For his plan to work Satan needs man's seed—and yes woman are already carrying these babies. They are being born and are even being snatched out of the womb. This is why we need to know about, become aware of and then divorce the spirit husbands and wives that are attached to our time lines and DNA structures. They impact our lives in so many areas. To learn more go and watch this teaching from Dr. Stella Immanuel: www.firepoweredministries.orghttp://www.youtube.com/watch?feature=player_ embedded&v=CJrJG9xymts#at=11

Are these babies flesh or spirit? The Nephilim are already living among us. They are super beings—a mixture of evil spirit and humanity—Satan once again copying YHVH's plan for man (His Spirit in us against Satan's spirit in us.) Have you noticed that everything in the shops are super human—Superman, Superwoman, Superpowers. Children are growing up with this mindset. Everywhere we see the changing of DNA: Dracula, zombies, (do you know how many people (children) are already programed as zombies?), vampires, werewolves, beasts, monsters, and aliens. Yes, Satan has sex slaves who willingly give their seed. But remember that even using your tongue to gossip builds his empire on earth.

Reflection:
* Do you live aware of what is going on around you?
* Remember there are only two kingdoms—Light and darkness—which do you serve?

Response:
Ask Holy Spirit to open your eyes so that you can see what is happening around you.

You belong to YHVH

Little children (believers, dear ones), you are of God and you belong to Him and have [already] overcome them [the agents of the antichrist]; because He who is in you is greater than he (Satan) who is in the world [of sinful mankind].

1 John 4:4 [AMPLIFIED BIBLE]

Yeshua was victorious and He paid the price so that we can be free. We do battle from a place of victory! But, you will only be able to fight this battle when you have died to self and begin seeing through the schemes and devices of the enemy. The final battle is NOW, this is why Satan continues destroying human DNA. He is building an army of self-lovers, a harlot bride, from all populations with a genetic code controlled by him. Then he can program them using mind-control so that people will submit to his and not Yeshua's will.

Ask yourself who controls your thoughts, your desires, your lusts, and your cold heart? Have you died to self-lust and submitted to Holy Spirit? Many of God's children cannot give a clear-cut answer. In some areas you may stand in victory, but in others you struggle, exalting self and your desires. This is genetic manipulation. Part of you loves Yeshua, but the mixed seed is programed to serve your self-god. Since Satan cannot create like YHVH, he tries to twist YHVH's creation, changing it into his likeness, and his end-times army. He will give you such a desire for sex that you masturbate and then he claims the seed! YHVH's Word teaches self-control, but he says, "You have needs, so help yourself, I need your seed!"

Reflection:

* Look around you, do you see the signs of the final battle?
* 1 John 4:4 says YHVH, who is in you is greater than Satan.

Response:

If you believe that YHVH is greater then tell Him.

Walk by the Spirit

So I say, walk by the Spirit, and you will not gratify the desires of the flesh.
Galatians 5:16

The second coming of the Messiah is drawing closer. This means Satan is working harder to keep people from the Truth. Sadly, he is succeeding, even with YHVH's children, because we still live in the flesh. We still want to work everything out in the flesh. For instance: Will there be a rapture, will we have immortal bodies, if so how will it all work? Ask Holy Spirit to guide and lead you in these things. But why do you worry it. Instead get your life in order because you are still in the flesh. You must be transparent as sons of God because He is coming for a pure bride.

The flesh cannot be argued out. Don't be consumed and side tracked by these things, they are of the spirit. We don't have the ability to fully understand YHVH's ways. I am sure it won't be like we think, expect or were taught. Aldo cont nually says Yeshua is on His way to fetch us. Two will sleep and one will be gone, make sure you are dead to the flesh and living in the Spirit! When I look at Aldo I see how YHVH uses the foolish to teach the wise. How He always uses the loser and not the winner, how He says lose your life and then you will find it again.

Reflection:
- Are you walking by the Spirit one hundred percent?
- If not what are you going to do about it?

Response:
Write down your reflections and spend time in YHVH's presence worshipping Him.

Becoming battle ready

'"He who has an ear, let him hear what the Spirit says to the churches. To him who overcomes I will give to eat from the tree of life, which is in the midst of the Paradise of God."'
Revelation 2:7 [NEW KING JAMES VERSION]

The enemy's darts are designed to make us fall, but we stand firm! Aldo explains daily through Holy Spirit (Wisdom) what is happening in the spirit. It is often a real challenge to me. They reveal a 'battleground,' but also prompt me to speak out—because if you know things—you have to speak out!

Victory comes through overcoming. And to be an overcomer—you need to overcome a challenge or a battle! I know Holy Spirit is raising up an army for Armageddon. So you, as the Bride of Yeshua, will be taught to fight. You will fight and pray, pray and fight for your family, just as Nehemiah taught us to do. I sometimes receive emails throwing darts at me. Some come from Christians who believe I am bewitching the body of Christ. Others come from Satanists angry because I am revealing Truth to the Body. Aldo wrote, "Mom, you need to cover yourself and remove the darts from your heart—because Jezebel in this person (....) is pouring acid on you with their words of accusation. They want to paralyze you. Wash it off with the Blood of Yeshua and forgive them. Mom, now you have to go to the Heavenly court and repent for yourself and your forefathers who spoke the same kind of evil words over men and woman of YHVH."

Reflection:
* If victory comes through overcoming then how are you doing?
* Don't allow the enemy's darts to keep you down. Rise up to fight another day.

Response:
Declare your intention to stand your ground and overcome in the Name of Yeshua, who will give you the victory.

Wear God's complete armor

Therefore, put on the complete armor of God, so that you will be able to [successfully] resist and stand your ground in the evil day [of danger], and having done everything [that the crisis demands], to stand firm [in your place, fully prepared, immovable, victorious].
Ephesians 6:13 [AMPLIFIED BIBLE]

I want to explain something to you today, and I believe Holy Spirit will teach you the fullness of this Truth. We all need to build the walls around our souls to protect them from the fiery darts of the enemy. But, if there are still judgements (un-repented sin) against you and your fore-fathers in the Heavenly courts, the principalities and powers in the air will know and use this to curse you because they know it will be effective.

Un-repented sin in your DNA is like Velcro—it will stick to whatever it touches. But, as you repent and receive the increased anointing of Holy Spirit (oil), and apply the Blood of the Lamb, your Velcro will become clean and nothing will be able to stick to it. This is the process of lifelong sanctification that I believe we must all be a part of. All the unsanctified areas of your life are the places where the familiar spirits of your family will still live in you. Their purpose is to keep you blind and deaf. They want to operate through you to harm the people around you and the body of Christ. You can be a Christian with the best intentions but Jezebel, Baal, and Liviathan will use these areas of your life to work through you to hurt others.

Reflection:
- Spend time in YHVH's presence allowing Holy Spirit to reveal any un-repented sin to you.
- Ask Holy Spirit to reveal any ancestors who's DNA might be infecting you.

Response:
Deal with whatever Holy Spirit reveals to you. Resolve with Holy Spirit's help to stand firm against the powers of darkness.

Battle in the Heavenly realm

For our struggle is not against flesh and blood [contending only with physical opponents], but against the rulers, against the powers, against the world forces of this [present] darkness, against the spiritual forces of wickedness in the heavenly (supernatural) places.
Ephesians 6:12 [AMPLIFIED BIBLE]

I see war being waged in people's lives! The Kingdom of YHVH operates differently from the kingdom of darkness. What looks like war to you Yeshua calls "healing." Until you are delivered of all your demons, and you are healed of your brokenness, you will not experience fullness. Aldo wrote the other day: "It is time for Lazarus to get out of the grave!" It takes time and effort to uproot a big tree. I have never seen a big tree being uprooted by just looking at it, or by simply hoping and trusting that it will disappear. Even Yeshua cursed the fig tree when He saw that it did not have any fruit.

The body of Christ is blinded by the demonic web over us. It blinds our eyes from seeing the truth. We think we are in His will only when everything is going well. I was so fast asleep all my life. I did not understand or know what being sanctified in the spirit meant or looked like, or that it involves a process. Do you really think that the familiar spirits who've been in your family for decades will just leave if there is darkness in you? Do you believe that they won't make a fuss when you start bringing in the Light and the Truth!

Reflection:
- Are you one of those people who believe that God's blessing equals lack of difficulties in your life?
- Do you realize against whom your struggle is?

Response:
What are you going to do about it?

Are you longing for revival?

However, I am telling you nothing but the truth when I say it is profitable (good, expedient, advantageous) for you that I go away. Because it I do not go away, the Comforter (Counselor, Helper, Advocate, Intercessor, Strengthener, Standby) will not come to you [into close fellowship with you]; but if I go away, I will send Him to you [to be in close fellowship with you].

John 16:7 [AMPLIFIED BIBLE CLASSIC]

And when He comes, He will convict and convince the world and bring demonstration to it about sin and about righteousness (uprightness of heart and right standing with God) and about judgment: About sin, because they do not believe in Me [trust in, rely on, and adhere to Me]; About righteousness (uprightness of heart and right standing with God), because I go to My Father, and you will see Me no longer; About judgment, because the ruler (evil genius, prince) of this world [Satan] is judged and condemned and sentence already is passed upon him. I have still many things to say to you, but you are not able to bear them or to take them upon you or to grasp them now. But when He, the Spirit of Truth (the Truth-giving Spirit) comes; He will guide you into all the Truth (the whole, full Truth). For He will not speak His own message [on His own authority]; but He will tell whatever He hears [from the Father; He will give the message that has been given to Him], and He will announce and declare to you the things that are to come [that will happen in the future]. He will honor and glorify Me, because He will take of (receive, draw upon) what is Mine and will reveal (declare, disclose, transmit) it to you. Everything that the Father has is Mine. That is what I meant when I said that He [the Spirit] will take the things that are Mine and will reveal (declare, disclose, transmit) it to you. (John 16:8-15 AMP).

Reflection:

*   Are you longing for revival?
*   What has Holy Spirit said to you as you read this Scripture? Think about what He has quickened in your Spirit.

Response:

Pray this portion of Scripture. Spending time on each phrase and allowing it to sink into your spirit.

The Refiner's fire

But who can endure the day of his coming? Who can stand when he appears?
For he will be like a refiner's fire or a launderer's soap.
Malachi 3:2

The baptism of the Holy Spirit and Fire will change your life forever. I know that YHVH is now sending fire upon His children so that we will be convicted to look at the condition of our hearts. I have experienced the power of His fire in my life. This is why I keep on asking Him to put His Fire in my wounds and all of my being! The more Fire, the more dirt and snakes come out. Now, like never before, we need to put our hands on our own hearts. We have to stop pointing a finger at everyone else. We need to take full responsibility for our lives and what is going on in our hearts.

YHVH is preparing His Bride to be ready for Yeshua's return. This is why you will experience and testify of the divine fire that came upon your life. But understand this, it is to clean your soul. YHVH and His Holy Spirit are like a Refining Fire. So many times we go through difficult situations, but remember the Fire is purifying us as we humble ourselves and repent before the King. Sometimes people go through difficulties, without being changed, this is because they are not allowing the Glory Light to shine into their lives. They choose not to fight the fight, but rather they want the easy solution.

Reflection:
* Where do you stand: Are you prepared to welcome the Refiners Fire in your life?
* Or do you want the easy solution?

Response:
Ask Holy Spirit to give you the courage to walk the walk, and fight the fight.

Armed for battle

You armed me with strength for battle; you humbled my adversaries before me.
You made my enemies turn their backs in flight, and I destroyed my foes.
Psalm 18:39-40

Trials can result from disobedience and sin in our lives. A stubborn hardened heart gives the enemy free access into our lives. YHVH's Fire can only come into this situation (this pain, this battle) when we repent from a place of humbleness, asking His Fire to come and burn and expose the snakes as well as the root of the problem. Many times people's hearts become hard as they go through trials, because they want the situation to be fixed without YHVH's Fire and His Blood. There are no shortcuts. Fire has the ability to change the form of everything! It can even change a stubborn, prideful heart into a humble gentle heart.

I have also seen that trials are like tests. In these fiery tests we will be led by Holy Spirit to stand, to go to Court in Heaven, to fight, to pray and to overcome the situation. Yeshua uses every trial that we surrender into His hands to make us grow in maturity. And at the end it always works together for our good. He uses all things, even our journey through the valley of death to show us that He will never leave us and never forsake us. He teaches our hands to war just like David's. He uses our trials to humble us and to make us experience His life changing Fire!

Reflection:
- You cannot do effective battle against the enemy with a stubborn, hardened heart.
- Whom do you trust in battle: YHVH or yourself?

Response:
Ask Yeshua to soften your heart so that you can be receptive to what YHVH is doing in your life.

Fiery trials

Dear friends, do not be surprised at the fiery ordeal that has come on you to test you, as though something strange were happening to you. But rejoice inasmuch as you participate in the sufferings of Christ, so that you may be overjoyed when his glory is revealed.
1 Peter 4:12-13

There were times in my life when I was in the midst of the Fire and everything within me burned. The humbling part of this process is that all the dirt inside of you is exposed by the Fire. It brought me to a place of repentance, and started me on the journey of dying to self. Yes, you "die" when you enter His Fire! But you are never alone, He is always with you. His Fire has a complete life changing effect. It brought me face to face with the King.

As you experience His Shekinah Glory, you will know that your life will never be the same. One second in His presence and you will "die." DIE TO SELF! It is the Fire that makes you completely transparent. Your whole being shouts out—Holy, Holy, Holy is He! His presence is always in that Fire. He is the all-consuming Fire. And the beauty is that He wants us to walk in that Fire, to be baptized with the Fire. To be immersed in the Fire, just as canned fruit is soaked in syrup. To be consumed by His Fire. Yeshua wants us to be so filled with His Holy Spirit and Fire that we can go out and do what He asks. Not in our own strength, but in His dunamis (miraculous) power.

Reflection:
* What is YHVH saying to you about your attitude toward walking through the Fire?
* Are you prepared to go to battle and die to self?

Response:
Write a prayer of worship to YHVH the all-consuming Fire who is Holy, Holy, Holy and all powerful.

War against fear

The Lord is my light and my salvation—whom shall I fear?
The Lord is the stronghold of my life—of whom shall I be afraid?
Psalm 27:1

The devil's favorite modus operandi is fear. Demons feed upon fear in the atmosphere. These are words of fear, the unhealed wounds in the soul filled with fear, the trauma memories filled with fear, the fear of rejection, the fear of failing or the fear of not being good enough. Through all these fears the demons are strengthened and they build up resistance to being expelled. The primary spiritual force that ejects demons out of people's lives is the force called "Faith in Yeshua." By and through Faith we live in His Light and Truth.

The starting point to dealing with our fears is taking responsibility for our double lives. I am referring to the secret double life that operates in your subconscious, keeping you trapped in darkness and lies—filled with all kinds of fear. People don't realize that this secret life is not so secret, it is actually seen in the natural through your actions and in the spirit through your thoughts. Our Faith in YHVH, starts with a love relationship with Him and is released through the spoken word and Anointing. The Authority behind the spoken word is the key to Biblical deliverance. It was Yeshua's spoken words that caused demons to fear and obey Him. Under the Anointing, a single spoken word can drive out a multitude of devils from a possessed person.

Reflection:

- Do you walk by Faith or by fear? You can only win the war when you walk by Faith.
- How is your love relationship with YHVH? This is the key to overcoming.

Response:

Write the thoughts from your time of reflection.

Exhilarated in the Spirit

In all the travels of the Israelites, whenever the cloud lifted from above the tabernacle, they would set out; but if the cloud did not lift, they did not set out—until the day it lifted. So the cloud of the Lord was over the tabernacle by day, and fire was in the cloud by night, in the sight of all the Israelites during all their travels.
Exodus 40:36-38

Humbly I bow down every day and thank Yeshua for our journey of Faith. I am excited and exhilarated in the Spirit. I believe that as we follow Holy Spirit He is leading us into new places. The enemy so badly wants to prevent us from entering these new places. Satan does this by keeping our minds in sin, by drawing us away from the things of God through that sin. The walk of sanctification will be vital in the time of preparation before YHVH releases His Spirit in a new way. He will do this through wonders, healings, and restorations. He will release these blessings upon all who are waiting upon Him to answer their prayers. Now is the time to prepare so that we will be ready.

When the cloud of His presence moves—we have to move with Him. Don't wait for your denomination to move; be ready to move with Holy Spirit! Leave the old behind, so that He can make all things new. Many will lose out because they hold on to their knowledge. God will give new instructions to His warriors. Align yourself with Him. Get fit. Get ready. Start praying, because the cloud is moving. Nothing will be the same as it was yesterday. Allow Holy Spirit to deposit a new thing in you—receive your blessings.

Reflection:
- Are you excited and exhilarated by Holy Spirit today?
- Examine your heart to see if there is anything that is holding you back from being ready to move forward with God.

Response:
Ask Holy Spirit to open the eyes of your spirit so that you can see what He wants you to pray for today.

The physical or the Spiritual?

He heals the brokenhearted and binds up their wounds.
Psalm 147:3

When I have my monthly chat box day my heart breaks. I hear stories from people around the world who phone in. I literally sit the entire day listening to people, and then I go down on my knees and I pray for them. They share their problems and the manifestations they experience. However so many of them do not understand that the battle is not in the physical, no, it is in the Spirit. Even though each person has a different story to tell, we all have the same "illness"—and that is a broken heart.

As a result I was led to write a book about it. I struggled to explain these things, because as I look around I see most people view life from the perspective of the flesh. They don't seem able to see in the Spirit. On my knees I prayed, *"Abba, You allowed us to walk this journey with Aldo, to see and understand so many things in the Spirit—but people fight these truths Lord, they fight them with all they have!"* When I discovered that I was wrong I realized it was my pride—the mixed seed in me—fighting the Truth! Are you fighting the fact that the spirit is true and real, and that your battle is not in the flesh, but in the spirit?

Reflection:

* As you contemplate this question, spend time in Abba's presence asking Him to reveal the state of your heart to you.
* Are you going to choose to believe in Him and allow Him to shine His Glory Light into your heart?

Response:

Write a prayer to Abba in response to what He has shown you.

Overcoming the world

These things I have spoken unto you, that in me ye might have peace. In the world ye shall have tribulation: but be of good cheer; I have overcome the world.
John 16:33 [KING JAMES VERSION]

We need to move into the Light; we need to face the truth about ourselves. Go on your knees, call out to YHVH, and invite Him into your darkness and pain. Then see how He restores Life and Light to you. I see so many marriages breaking up because of the "double" that lives in people. Aldo and Chantelle are walking this walk of purification that we all should have walked before we got married. You can say, "I did not choose the pain, the brokenness through which Satan works in me." That might be true but this is why Yeshua died for you and me, He knew this and wanted to set you free.

I look at Paul and how he appealed for the deliverance of his soul from the spiritual opposition and warfare that worked contrary to the true desire of his heart. So today I say "Thanks be to YHVH through Yeshua my King, we can all be free and experience victory in this battle as we surrender to the fortifying work of YHVH." If you choose Light, you will be called an "overcomer." You will be part of Yeshua's overcoming victorious army who inherit the great promises reserved specifically for those who choose Life. Our grace is the impartation of His heart—our desire to be fully submitted to the will of our Father.

Reflection:
* Have you invited YHVH into your darkness and your pain?
* You will not be able to embark on the journey of moving from the darkness into the Light until you do.

Response:
Choose what you are going to do and then write a prayer to YHVH expressing the desires of your heart.

You are the gatekeeper

I see a complete lack of understanding in parents with regards to protecting their children in the spiritual realm. Why do I need to be my children's spiritual gatekeeper—aren't they accountable for themselves? In Hosea we read that: My people are destroyed from lack of knowledge. We so desperately need spiritual discernment. Today, like never before, there is a raging battle at the gates of families, all to get to our children. Spiritual gates are portals and entry ways into people, families, groups, nations, business etc.

When I fly, there is someone who looks at my ticket—they are the gatekeepers. They keep everyone off the plane without a ticket or who would cause harm. In 1 Chronicles 9:17-27 we read that the gatekeepers were appointed and chosen by the King. They had a daily responsibility which was the safety of the temple. They had to be loyal and trustworthy. So often children say to me, "I cannot trust my parents, look at what they have done, and they were supposed to protect me." Children know your spiritual calling as a gatekeeper, sometimes better than you do. Gates and walls are there for protection. What do our gates as parents look like? What is allowed to enter and exit through your gates?

Reflection:

* Think on the two questions at the end of paragraph two.
* What are your answers to these questions?

Response:

Ask Yeshua to help you to be a diligent gatekeeper for your family.

Gatekeeper and spiritual warrior

Your gates will always stand open, they will never be shut, day or night, so that people may bring you the wealth of the nations—their kings led in triumphal procession.
Isaiah 60:11

Not only are we the gatekeepers of our children's lives, but also of our own gates. We need to be aware of what comes in through our "ear gates," "eye gates," "mouth gate," even our "nose gates" (inhalation of drugs). Are you at your post daily? The gates have purpose and meaning. As in the natural, they can allow or prevent entry and exit. They can confine, shut down, and control spiritual traffic. In Isaiah chapter 60 we see the church rising up, taking authority to facilitate the harvest. Verse 11 says that in the midst of the harvest the gates open so that the harvest can come in. I see control at the gate. That is where the provision of YHVH enters.

YHVH had a plan, and that is that we as parents would be our children's gatekeepers, their watchmen. We need to take up our position at the gate. We are the gatekeepers and spiritual warriors. We must be aware that if we choose to keep the gate open with anger, pornography, hate or unforgiveness, this is what will enter, and what our children will have to deal with and experience. We are called to be watchmen and gatekeepers. I have to be the one who intercedes, who provides a safe place for my family through my life of right standing with YHVH.

Reflection:
* Are you being a watchful gatekeeper and a fierce spiritual warrior?
* What are you allowing to enter through the gates into your family?

Response:
Ask YHVH to forgive you for your lack of watchfulness.

Gates of Righteousness

Open to me the gates of righteousness; I will go through them, and I will praise the Lord. This is the gate of the Lord, through which the righteous shall enter.
Psalm 118:19-20

I have to understand that that which I ALLOW THROUGH MY GATE, IS WHAT MY CHILDREN WILL EXPERIENCE. When I enter into darkness, I pass that same oppression over to my children. Can children fight this? Off course, and it is a constant fight for children whose parents live in denial. Why make it so hard or them if you can help them through repentance and righteousness?

By understanding the purpose of gates we can redeem them for ourselves and our children to be portals of Life. Gates are a place of worship: *Enter his gates with thanksgiving and his courts with praise* (Psalm 100:4a). Gates are a place of warfare: *and your descendants shall possess the gate of their enemies* (Genesis 22:17b NKJV). Those who hate you also have gates: *And may your descendants possess the gates of those who hate them* (Genesis 24:60b NKJV). Scripture also tells us about the: Gates of Heaven—Genesis 28:17. Gates of righteousness—Psalm 118:19 Gates of hell—Matthew 16:18. Gates of the soul—Luke 22:3. Gates of the heart—Revelation 3:20. See your life in the spirit as a city. Without order, walls and gates it can hardly be considered a city. Without these structures it will be open for the enemy to attack you, your children and ungodly influences will have constant free access.

Reflection:
- YHVH has called you to be a Gate of Righteousness that will protect your children.
- Ask YHVH to help you to fulfill this important role faithfully.

Response:
Commit yourself before YHVH to fighting the battle against darkness in the spiritual realm.

Light in the darkness

The Light shines on in the darkness, and the darkness did not understand it or overpower it or appropriate it or absorb it [and is unreceptive to it].
John 1:5 [AMPLIFIED BIBLE]

Darkness cannot enter Light; no demon can withstand YHVH's Light. So when you understand the power of His Light, and also the power of darkness you will begin to understand the power in taking full responsibility for your mistakes. This starts by acknowledging that I am wrong and inviting Holy Spirit into my pain. The realm of the Light allows us to live in safety, to receive His blessings and to experience His power through us. When we walk in the Light, we choose the exposure of darkness in us so that healing and restoration can start. Yeshua wants us to be one with the Light, completely transparent, acknowledging who we are so that He can be who He is—our Savior, Healer and Redeemer.

But if we walk in the light, as he is in the light ...the blood of Jesus, his Son, purifies us from all sin (1 John 1:7). Walking in the Light means walking in YHVH's Word—from Genesis to Revelation. We are transformed through YHVH's words of Life and Light. Reading the Word switches on the Light inside of you. The Truth becomes more than mere knowledge, it becomes Light and Life to you. This only happens to those who receive the Truth of YHVH into their very substance and they carry the fruit of light instead of the fruit of darkness.

Reflection:

- You have the choice of either being a vessel that carries Light or one that carries darkness.
- The only way to fight and win at spiritual warfare is to have the Light shining within you.

Response:

Allow Holy Spirit to minister to you as you commit yourself to YHVH and His Word of Life and Light.

*Therefore, I urge you, brothers and sisters,
in view of God's mercy,
to offer your bodies as a living sacrifice,
holy and pleasing to God—
this is your true and proper worship.
Do not conform to the pattern of this world,
but be transformed by the renewing of your mind.
Then you will be able to test
and approve what God's will is—
his good, pleasing and perfect will.*
Romans 12:1-2

Renew your mind

Those who live according to the flesh
have their minds set on what the flesh desires;
but those who live in accordance with the Spirit
have their minds set on what the Spirit desires.
The mind governed by the flesh is death,
but the mind governed by the Spirit is life and peace.
Romans 8:5-6

To be made new in the attitude of your minds;
and to put on the new self,
created to be like God in true righteousness and holiness.
Ephesians 4:23-24

Renewed day by day

Therefore we do not lose heart.
Though outwardly we are wasting away, yet inwardly we are being renewed day by day.
2 Corinthians 4:16

Are you believing Satan's lies about you and your circumstances? Are you stuck in ungodly beliefs, instead of believing what your Abba says about you? If so you are leaving the door wide open for Satan to come in and control your mind. He does this step-by-step. Your mind is the battleground. Once you see the truth of this you can be set free!!! The Word says that the Truth sets you free. I started to pray the Glory Light over Aldo's mind. ..."*I am the light of the world. Whoever follows me will never walk in darkness, but will have the light of life*" (John 8:12). Satan's lies shackle us so that we are prevented from living an Abundant Life.

One of the most beautiful things is when Yeshua shows up in the midst of one of Satan's lies and reveals the truth. Instantly that person receives freedom and often healing as well. There are times though that the lie is so deep, and been repeated so often that only Holy Spirit can lift it out of the subconscious. The war is between the truth and the lies. An unbelieving heart is a sinful heart. It cannot be obedient because it is controlled by the old nature and the flesh. Unbelief makes God a liar. But, God is faithful, you can take Him at His word.

Reflection:

- Is your mind a battleground, and if so who is winning?
- Ask Abba to reveal to you all your ungodly beliefs.

Response:

Respond by writing down the ungodly beliefs that Holy Spirit reveals to you. Next to each one write a declaration of belief based on what God says about you and your circumstances.

A sound mind

Strip yourselves of your former nature [put off and discard your old unrenewed self] which characterized your previous manner of life and becomes corrupt through lusts and desires that spring from delusion; And be constantly renewed in the spirit of your mind [having a fresh mental and spiritual attitude], And put on the new nature (the regenerate self) created in God's image, [Godlike] in true righteousness and holiness.
Ephesians 4:22-24 [THE AMPLIFIED BIBLE CLASSIC EDITION]

People use the excuse, "God knows my heart—He knows I cannot stop sinning". What god do you serve? The god of this world is the spirit that is at work in the hearts of those who refuse to obey God (Ephesians 2:2). The most High God gave you His Spirit of Life and it overrules the spirit of death in us (Romans 8). So, when we are faced with a temptation, we should call out to Him for His help, and His Spirit within us will come to our aid.

We have to fight the temptations and walk in Holiness. We all still make mistakes but we have Holy Spirit to help us in everything, even to say no to sin. Through this we will recognize and recognize the lies from our flesh in our minds and will be able to deal with them! Don't be deceived, Satan would like to hang a plaque around your neck: Double life? Immaturity? Greed? Selfish? Lust, or pride? Which are you? Let's stand up, remove these shackles and start renewing our minds, walking in victory! Knowing about YHVH's grace will not make you choose the right way. You need to have the mind of Christ; a sound mind, a pure heart and a love for Him that leaves you no choice but to obey Him in all He asks of you!

Reflection:
* Do you have a label that Satan has hung around your neck—if so what does it say?
* Which is it for you: Knowing about YHVH or having the mind of Christ?

Response:
Write a prayer asking Yeshua to give you His mind: A sound mind, a pure heart and a love for Him.

Follow the cloud

In all the travels of the Israelites, whenever the cloud lifted from above the tabernacle, they would set out; but if the cloud did not lift, they did not set out—until the day it lifted.
Exodus 40:36-37

When the blessings is poured out in the gates only a few who will receive it because many are still fighting over the doctrine of man. Avoid people who want to tie you up in arguments. You must do everything in His Spirit. If you are not willing to walk in the Spirit you will not be able to see and follow the cloud. It is a new place of victory in Him. From there we will fight like Debora in the 'Heavenlies.' (This is what we are starting to teach in the Spirit School).

It is all about generational change—you must pray, cleansing your time line and the sound portals that have been defiled over the generations. This is one of the reasons why you don't hear God's voice. You are the one who needs to open up your generational wells. You must open new wells with Holy Spirit. It is all about a new understanding that brings with it a heartfelt cry—why did I never believe that I needed my spiritual senses to be opened? You will not see or experience without them being cleaned and your mind renewed. As you stand in the gates you will see all the earth is ready and those who take up their places will all be in a place where they will renew their first love.

Reflection:
- Are you standing in the gates or are you caught up with the arguments of man?
- What must you do so that you are free to follow the Cloud when the Spirit moves?

Response:
Journal what Holy Spirit is revealing to you about opening your generational wells?

The mind of Yeshua

Let this mind be in you which was also in Christ Jesus.
Philippians 2:5 [NEW KING JAMES VERSION]

*I*f *my people, who are called by my name, will humble themselves and pray and seek my face and turn from their wicked ways, then I will hear from heaven, and I will forgive their sin and will heal their land* (2 Chronicles 7:14). A few years ago I attended Dr Howard Morgan's conference (Panim el Panim) in Atlanta Georgia. How wonderful to meet so many people who seek to meet YHVH face to face. I cannot help wondering why it is that not many people experience His love tangibly. People try to find Him through knowledge and works, but He is found in love and humbleness. For some reason this is very difficult for people to understand.

Let this mind be in you which was also in Christ Jesus, who, being in the form of God, did not consider it robbery to be equal with God, but made Himself of no reputation, taking the form of a bondservant (Philippians 2:5-7a NEW KING JAMES VERSION). What is it that makes us so proud? Is it our money, our houses, our reputation or our popularity? Is it people's opinion of us? Or is it simply that whenever you go everybody takes notice of you because of your knowledge, your beauty and your money?

Reflection:
* When last did you tangibly feel Yehsua's love in your life? What do you think is standing in the way of you experiencing His love?
* Where do you place your trust—in the things mentioned in the reading or in Yeshua.

Response:
Write your reactions to this reading and answers to the Reflection questions.

The renewed mind is humble

And being found in appearance as a man, He humbled Himself and became obedient to the point of death, even the death of the cross.
Philippians 2:8 [NEW KING JAMES VERSION]

Let's look at Yeshua, was He popular? Isaiah 53:3a says, *He was despised and rejected by mankind, a man of suffering, and familiar with pain.* In Luke 6:26 we read that Jesus said, *"Woe to you when everyone speaks well of you, for that is how their ancestors treated the false prophets."* The disciples were not above their Master. Yeshua was despised and rejected by man. The world cast Him out. So, why are we so filled with pride about who we are and what we do? Yeshua did not even boast about His learning or education. No, the Word says, Let this mind be in you, which was also in Yeshua.

He humbled Himself and took on the form of a servant. The night in the Upper room Yeshua took a towel and washed the Disciple's feet. We are so often ashamed to do the lowly jobs. But Yeshua keeps on saying to me "Retah, let this mind be in you—the mind of a bondservant! Don't try to be "Someone", Retah, be My hands, and My feet—nothing else." That is what Wisdom asks of Aldo, every day. And I want to tell you, the religious spirit hates humbleness, because it doesn't fit in with man's doctrine that says let's boast in who we are.

Reflection:
*   Where do you rate on the humility scale?
*   Read Philippians 2:5-8 again.

Response:
What is Yeshua saying to you about humility today?

Meditate on His Word

One thing I have asked of the Lord, and that I will seek: That I may dwell in the house of the Lord [in His presence] all the days of my life, to gaze upon the beauty [the delightful loveliness and majestic grandeur] of the Lord and to meditate in His temple.
Psalm 27:4 [AMPLIFIED BIBLE]

On chat box days many people talk to me about prayer. "Retah, why doesn't YHVH answer my prayers?" Yeshua hears all your prayers; you have to hear what I say to you today. Yeshua hears and listens to all your prayers—every word. He knows about every tear you pour out at His feet! Make sure you come into His rest, be content and find peace in knowing that He knows exactly what you need, and when you need it. Often in my life I have prayed and not receive. Then I found that when I prayed and asked Him for His Kingdom to come into the situation everything worked out for my good. Maybe not as I thought or wanted it, but I am at peace knowing that He is in control. I am content wanting only His perfect will and Kingdom to come in my life and every situation.

We seek many things in life. A new job, a house, a car, maybe answers, but when last did you seek His face? David was a great King. He was rich, he had won many battles and he had a great reputation. Yet he said, *One thing I ask from the Lord, this only do I seek: ... to gaze on the beauty of the Lord and to seek him in his temple.*

Reflection:
* What do you mainly pray about and what is the result?
* Do you have the peace of knowing that YHVH is in control of your life?

Response:
Pray Psalm 27:4 and write down your thoughts and desires as you pray it.

A form of godliness

We need to come to a place where we understand the true abundant love of our King. That He and He alone can save us through His Blood. Then we will be so thankful and in love with Him that we will move towards ultimate closeness with Him. We will choose Holiness, and the road of sanctification. In that place we will experience the reality of His peace, protection, provision, joy and love in His presence. As we repent of our double lives we enter intimately into His glorious presence and His Glory Light stays in us to expose the devices and schemes of Satan.

The Cross, personal Salvation, baptism of Holy Spirit and the indwelling Spirit of Christ in us are the foundational building blocks of the overcomer's life. The reality of YHVH's Kingdom "now." His kingdom patterns and discerning of Truth from the lies allow us to see where we are and what changes we need to make. Yeshua the Anointed One is our source of power for change in our hearts and lives. I do encounter many people who do not like hearing these Truths. But, I am so sorry, I am not called to tell you the things that tickle your ears. I share only what Yeshua is revealing through His Spirit to Aldo now in this hour.

Reflection:
* As you examine your heart today what is YHVH saying to you through Holy Spirit?
* Are you living your life having a form of godliness but denying its power?

Response:
Open your heart up to Holy Spirit today, allowing the Glory Light to shine into your heart.

Love overcomes fear

There is no fear in love [dread does not exist]. But perfect (complete, full-grown) love drives out fear, because fear involves [the expectation of divine] punishment, so the one who is afraid [of God's judgment] is not perfected in love [has not grown into a sufficient understanding of God's love].

1 John 4:18 [AMPLIFIED BIBLE]

It is the Anointing that breaks the yoke. Yeshua wants us to handle the manifestations of anger or fear in people by manifesting the opposite spirit. When you come in the same evil spirit—fighting anger with anger—nothing will happen. Can Satan drive out Satan? No. It is Christ in us, who is Light, Truth, and Love. It is Holy Spirit in us who brings the Anointing.

When I reach the place of real repentance the demonic forces cannot return into my life. They cannot re-enter because I have begun living in the Light of Christ, and it is impossible for them to survive there. The manifest presence of Holy Spirit and the Word of YHVH causes real torment for demons. Bondages and strongholds over the mind are not only dealt with by deliverance but also through the renewing of the mind. This is done by dealing with the pain and the lies inside our painful memories. We need healing in our pain and sorrows. By facing the pain, working through the memories and seeing the experiences in the Light of His Truth, lies can be exposed and His love and faithfulness can bring us out of bondage. The Truth shall set you free and will enable your mind to be renewed and aligned with the mind of Christ.

Reflection:
- Have you allowed YHVH to begin healing your pain and sorrow?
- The only way to receive lasting healing is through the renewing of your mind.

Response:
Spend some time journaling your fears and anger. Then bring them to YHVH and deal with them in the Light of His Truth.

Don't copy the world

Therefore, I urge you, brothers and sisters, in view of God's mercy, to offer your bodies as a living sacrifice, holy and pleasing to God—this is your true and proper worship.
Romans 12:1

Paul begs us in Romans (the Amplified Bible puts this so well). *Therefore I urge you, brothers and sisters, by the mercies of God, to present your bodies [dedicating all of yourselves, set apart] as a living sacrifice, holy and well-pleasing to God, which is your rational (logical, intelligent) act of worship. And do not be conformed to this world [any longer with its superficial values and customs], but be transformed and progressively changed [as you mature spiritually] by the renewing of your mind [focusing on godly values and ethical attitudes], so that you may prove [for yourselves] what the will of God is, that which is good and acceptable and perfect [in His plan and purpose for you]* (12:1-2 AMPLIFIED BIBLE).

We mentally curse people because of our own prejudices. The key to finding YHVH's will for our lives is by offering ourselves as a living sacrifice to Him. The problem is that most people don't even see that they have given themselves and their money as a living sacrifice to Satan. To give yourself to Yeshua means making yourself totally available to Him as a servant. In this process He renews your mind and your heart, then Holy Spirit takes control of your life. As your thought life changes you will start walking in the good, pleasing and perfect will of YHVH for your life.

Reflection:

- Meditate on Romans 12:1-2 asking Holy Spirit to speak to you about your commitment to Yeshua.
- Open yourself up to the ministry of Holy Spirit into your life.

Response:

Pray through Romans 12:1-2.

Your Word is Truth

Sanctify them by the truth; your word is truth.
John 17:17

Walking in the Light is walking in the Truth, and that means walking in the Life of YHVH. So when you pray for people who are in darkness, pray the Light of YHVH into their darkness! Declare YHVH's Light over all darkness: Your own, your children's and your families' darkness! It will begin manifesting because it cannot stand in the Light of YHVH. You want this to happen because if it doesn't come out now, it will feed on and hide behind the evil darkness still inside, sprouting mixed seeds.

Yeshua wants a pure bride. In His Light all the hidden secrets and darkness are revealed. All your evil seed in your foundation will be exposed. I see how when people have never dealt with their sin, the same sin recurs at the same age in their children. So, for e.g. at the same time you started having sexual relationships outside of marriage, your kids will start. It is as if this un-repented sin is like a magnet that draws your offspring to do exactly what you did. That is what happens when you don't deal with the evil seed in your foundations. These evil seeds are things like adultery, financial dishonesty, bitterness and un-forgiveness in your heart. All of these will be exposed when people start praying the Glory Light of YHVH over situations.

Reflection:
* Spend time before Holy Spirit allowing Him to examine your heart.
* What do you find inside of yourself: Light or darkness?

Response:
Ask YHVH to cleanse your heart and shine His Glory Light deep into you so that all sin can be cleaned out.

Taking thoughts captive

The weapons we fight with are not the weapons of the world. On the contrary, they have divine power to demolish strongholds. We demolish arguments and every pretension that sets itself up against the knowledge of God, and we take captive every thought to make it obedient to Christ.

2 Corinthians 10:4-5

Romans 12:2 tells us not to be conformed to this world. I see how people all want deliverance, but what they do not understand is that you need some substance in your spirit. I am speaking of having the Word of YHVH, Truth, Faith and Love as building blocks. You need to build your life upon the Word of YHVH to have permanent results, if not you will be in need of constant deliverance and/or therapy. Love the Word of YHVH, read it, eat it, let your spirit, soul and body feed upon it. Ask Yeshua to give you a hunger for His Word that is greater than your desire for food!

So many people live in oppression, obsession and possession by demons as a result of their thought life. When I say possessed by demons you have to understand this means all the areas in your life that: Are in and operate out of darkness—dark words, dark angry and hateful thoughts, bitterness, and jealousy, these are all filled with demons. Holy Spirit only lives in the areas of your soul that are flooded by Light and Truth. You might ask how you can change this: Through repentance you trade them for Life—His Zoe Life inside of you. His Light gives real Life. You will have the nature of your Abba and live in complete peace.

Reflection:
* Have you been going about the renewing of your mind in the wrong way?
* What did you learn from the piece you read today?

Response:
Write out a battle plan of how you are going to approach the renewing of your mind.

Don't be double-minded

Submit yourselves, then, to God. Resist the devil, and he will flee from you. Come near to God and he will come near to you. Wash your hands, you sinners, and purify your hearts, you double-minded.

James 4:7-8

When you shout, scream and gossip—it is not Yeshua—but the nature of Satan still in your darkness and pain that lashes out. That nature wants to find fault in everyone except you. Self-righteousness is flesh and it all starts with thoughts. The problem is that you do not want to face your pain, and now you hide behind the masks of coping and self-righteousness. Families break up and relationships crumble because people's minds are in darkness and they do not want to take responsibility for their thought lives and the resulting actions. Children are broken because of what parents hold onto, gladly passing it on as a legacy.

Your old thoughts and patterns of thinking must be removed from your life. We should guard our thought life and not allow weaknesses and the lust of the flesh to control them. I have found the treasure of acknowledging my mistakes, taking responsibility for my life, not blaming others, but asking Holy Spirit to search my heart and deal with the darkness and pain still in my subconscious. What good is it to keep on hiding behind "everyone is wrong, only I'm right?" That is what the enemy wants, because denial keeps you in darkness. This makes you double-minded and as the Word says, you will always be unstable in your ways.

Reflection:
* Whose nature are you exhibiting in your life?
* Have you taken responsibility for your own darkness or are you still blaming other people?

Response:
Repent and ask YHVH to renew your double mind.

Renew your mind

Finally, believers, whatever is true, whatever is honorable and worthy of respect, whatever is right and confirmed by God's word, whatever is pure and wholesome, whatever is lovely and brings peace, whatever is admirable and of good repute; if there is any excellence, if there is anything worthy of praise, think continually on these things [center your mind on them, and implant them in your heart].
Philippians 4:8 [AMPLIFIED BIBLE]

We need to repent and be rid of our wrong thoughts. Satan cannot read our minds. All the information he has about us is gained through our words, and our actions that speak louder than words. We either have a radiance in the spirit or we have a lack of it. I am referring to the brightness or darkness of the cloak you wear in the spirit realm that reflects your thoughts. It is this that gives him a clue as to the condition of your inner man. This is what he reacts to and uses against you.

The enemy wants to create a mental block or stronghold over your mind. This means you believe his lies and start living that way. You do not bother to find out the truth, you believe that you are always right and everyone else is wrong. You start living your own little dark life in your subconscious where you are controlled by what the demons ask you to do. I sometimes cannot believe how the enemy manages to keep people trapped in denial as they refuse to acknowledge the condition of their souls. In the book of Proverbs we read: *For as he thinks in his heart, so is he [in behavior—one who manipulates]* (23:7a AMP).

Reflection:

* Do you wear a cloak of Light or darkness in the spirit realm?
* How committed are you to finding out the truth—or are you happy to live trapped in denial?

Response:

Pray Philippians 4:8 asking Holy Spirit to shine Yeshua's Glory Light into your mind.

Guard your thoughts

I have come as Light into the world, so that everyone who believes and trusts in Me [as Savior—all those who anchor their hope in Me and rely on the truth of My message] will not continue to live in darkness.
John 12:46 [AMPLIFIED BIBLE]

Entrance to a soul is through the thoughts. It is very easy to command demons to come out, but it takes time to seal the gates into the thought life that they have used for such a long time. The thoughts have created a path in you and your body, soul and spirit remember it. So every time I feel like someone is rejecting me, my whole being goes back to the painful thoughts of my wounds and I once again open up to the dark thoughts that house the demons.

This will continue until the day I choose to change my focus from those who rejected me, to Yeshua, and begin inviting Him into my wounds to bring healing and forgiveness through His Light and Truth. Only then will I be able to see the judgments in my heart against people—the hate, bitterness and jealousy. I will start dealing with my own pain. Usually it isn't what people have done to us but our own pain that keeps us focused upon hating them. It is harder to break mental habits than physical habits. They create a stronger bondage than prison bars ever could. I have seen that people sometimes don't need deliverance for hours, no, they only need the truth about themselves and about Yeshua. Only Holy Spirit can bring that truth.

Reflection:
- If the entrance to your soul is through your thoughts what are you doing to guard them?
- Have you moved your focus from people to Yeshua?

Response:
Ask Yeshua to turn your hate, bitterness and jealously into love, joy and contentment.

Perfect love casts out fear

There is no fear in love; but perfect love casts out fear, because fear involves torment.
But he who fears has not been made perfect in love.
1 John 4:18 [NEW KING JAMES VERSION]

The power of YHVH's Love is greater than any "words" or "works" of man. How I rejoice in my Righteous Father's love. His love has the greatest healing power. Every problem in the soul of man can be healed by the revelation of the love of YHVH. Our souls can never function perfectly and be restored until we have an understanding of the true acceptance and healing that His love brings.

Our souls are filled with wounds and these are most often filled with demonic influences or sicknesses that are hidden in the subconscious. But, we are given a choice—either you choose to live with the wounds and live a broken life, or you can choose YHVH's Truth and allow His Glory Light to shine into your wounds and bring about healing. He washes our wounds and heals them with his Blood and Truth completely setting us free. As I move around I meet so many people who are so, so very broken. When I meet them I can say, "I know what it is like. I have been there." I can speak out of personal experience on how the enemy used Aldo's wounds to try to kill him with various sicknesses and lies that were told to him by the enemy.

Reflection:
- Are you renewing your mind based on the truth that YHVH loves you unconditionally?
- Or are you believing the enemy's lies that he tells you?

Response:
Pray to YHVH thanking Him for His unconditional love towards you. Allow His love to cast out all your fears.

Building His Kingdom

"This, then, is how you should pray: "'Our Father in heaven, hallowed be your name, your kingdom come, your will be done, on earth as it is in heaven.'"
Matthew 6:9-10

What are your goals, your dreams? This can be anything from your own selfish goals to have fame and wealth or a big ministry? You see, your goals (dreams) are stones that you use to build a kingdom. Are you busy building YHVH's kingdom or your own? There will be a day when the King of Glory will ask us, "Whose kingdom were you building with all your lies?" Please Yeshua, shake our man-made kingdoms!

Only when you understand His love for you, will you be able to lay all your lies and masks down for His Glory so that you can build His Kingdom here on earth. You will understand life and love. You will understand that every time we impart love, we are imparting life to those receiving our unconditional love. *"...'Man shall not live on bread alone, but on every word that comes from the mouth of God'"* (Matthew 4:4). YHVH is Love and every word that He speaks tells of His love for us. As I have watched Aldo and Chantelle, I have seen YHVH's beautiful process as He revealed all the darkness and lies in their wounds. He does the same for each of us if we will let Him. In these wounds are angry thoughts, lies, painful memories, and words or the wrong motives of our hearts.

Reflection:
* Have you asked yourself recently whose kingdom you are building?
* Are you receiving your main spiritual sustenance from the Word of God?

Response:
Ask Holy Spirit to help you to align your motives, thoughts, desires and goals with building YHVH's Kingdom.

A mind open to YHVH's love

The Word became flesh and made his dwelling among us. We have seen his glory, the glory of the one and only Son, who came from the Father, full of grace and truth.
John 1:14

The Word became flesh because He wanted us to know that He would never, ever leave us nor forsake us. How can love be known, unless it makes its home within us? Have you ever felt this love? It is a gentle love that covers the greatest pain. You can close your eyes and drink of this perfect love. Be still and know that this love is there for you as well. How can this true love grow, unless it is willing to sow with tears?

This is how I know it is true love—YHVH did not withhold His only Son. How do I know that my love for Him is true? I am willing to let go of all that I "love" for love of Him. This is how I know His grace, He demonstrated His love in such a way that we would never be able to say "I could not see it." He wanted us to feel His love; He wanted us to see it, to believe in it, to touch it and to breathe it. It is all that will sustain you during trials. His love is perfect. When you show REAL love, your heart is totally exposed. That is what He did on the Cross with arms wide open and a heart totally exposed—He showed us the greatest love.

Reflection:
* A mind renewed will be open to experiencing the love that YHVH offers to you.
* Be still and allow His love to flood your heart.

Response:
Ask Him today to open your mind and heart to receive from Him.

The greatest love

And he passed in front of Moses, proclaiming,"The Lord, the Lord, the compassionate and gracious God, slow to anger, abounding in love and faithfulness, maintaining love to thousands, and forgiving wickedness, rebellion and sin.
Exodus 34:6-7a

YHVH has displayed the greatest love—His perfect love for you and me. This love has overtaken my soul and all my fears disappear in His love. So by faith in His perfect love for me, I walk even when I don't see the road ahead of me. I climb even if I don't know how I will be able to breathe at that altitude. I trust even though it doesn't make sense, I hold on even though my hands are dead and I cannot feel the rope between my fingers. Yes, I hold onto my faith in Him, even if my eyes are blurred with overwhelming emotions. His love for me and His breath in me are all that keeps me moving forward.

So, the Word became flesh and made His home within me... So, the Word became flesh and made His home within me. I can say it over and over all day long. I feel Him so close to me because I know that He has made His home within me! No matter where I find myself in the world I know that I am never ever alone, because Yeshua is inside of me. This is the sweetest thing; there is nothing that His great love cannot fix! You just need to give your all to Him.

Reflection:
- Open your mind and your spirit to grasp the reality of what YHVH's love for you means.
- Don't sell yourself short as His child by not living in the fullness of His love for you.

Response:
Ask Holy Spirit to guide you into a full and complete understanding of YHVH's great love for you.

A sound mind

For God has not given us a spirit of fear,
but of power and of love and of a sound mind.
2 Timothy 1:7 [NEW KING JAMES VERSION]

There is a tangible spirit of fear hanging over many countries today and this needs to be overcome. People's feelings and emotions are running high. As I speak to people I can hear that they feel out of control. The News confronts us every day with increasing evidence that the world is out of control. Families are out of control, lawlessness is out of control and divorces have outnumbered marriages. When they are overwhelmed by their situations people retreat into something that appears to be safe, a place of hiding or escaping.   How do your children cope with all this fear and chaos? It is sad to see that not only children, but everyone is struggling with these feelings.

I see people slipping and escaping into their inner worlds where it is dark and filled with lies. One just has to look at the worldwide increase of people suffering from depression to know this is true. People use drugs or alcohol to numb the pain. Because of all this chaos and stress, people end up trapped in their subconscious with lies from which they feel they will never be set free. This is Satan's greatest lie because Yeshua has come to set you free and heal your broken heart. I will not stop proclaiming the Good News to those who have an ear to hear.

Reflection:
* Are you fearful, and if so what affect is it having on your life right now?
* You have to choose whether you will remain trapped in your fear or take the freedom Yeshua offers.

Response:
Choose freedom and ask YHVH to give you the sound mind that He promised you.

YHVH wants all of you

I beseech you therefore, brethren, by the mercies of God, that you present your bodies a living sacrifice, holy, acceptable to God, which is your reasonable service. And do not be conformed to this world, but be transformed by the renewing of your mind, that you may prove what is that good and acceptable and perfect will of God.
Romans 12:1-2 [NEW KING JAMES VERSION]

Do you know that Yeshua is constantly, gently knocking at the door of your heart? He is asking of you, "Give Me more of your time; give Me more of yourself, more of your heart. I want ALL of you." The degree to which we give of our hearts is the degree to which we receive. The darkness in our hearts and minds makes us hard-hearted, and then we cannot hear His voice. A hardened heart is a cursed heart. A hardened heart blames everyone else, never asks forgiveness and is not accountable for their actions. It is always about you and you alone. You do not understand the bigger picture—remember it is all about YHVH and His Kingdom.

Yeshua wants us to have fellowship with Him. He wants me completely for Himself—being dependent on Him alone, obeying Him in everything, being completely in love with Him. He is the one who draws near to me, a sinner. He is love eternal and is constantly aware of me and He desires my love and fellowship. Yes, He longs for you and me! And He created man to hear His voice. The more I acknowledge Him in me, the more I realize I cannot escape Him. He is the very air that I breathe.

Reflection:
* YHVH wants all of you: Body, soul and spirit. He wants your heart and He wants you mind.
* Are you able to give Him all of yourself or are you holding back?

Response:
Ask Holy Spirit to reveal to you what is causing the blockage in your life preventing you from surrendering whole-heartedly.

The Fountain of Life

How precious is Your lovingkindness, O God! Therefore the children of men put their trust under the shadow of Your wings. They are abundantly satisfied with the fullness of Your house, and You give them drink from the river of Your pleasures. For with You is the fountain of life; in Your light we see light.
Psalm 36:7-9 [NEW KING JAMES VERSION]

His presence in me is constantly growing. He urges me to seek Him and to drink from His Fountain of Life. The reward for seeking Him is a sense of His loving presence like never before. His presence is ever increasing in me as I give more and more of my heart to Him. His love burns like a fire. His love is far more intense than any human love. Yeshua is pure LOVE and the more time we spend with Him, the more our spiritual senses begin opening up. We begin to see that it is never about us, but only always about Him. He asks us to lay down everything that we love more than we love Him, and to give up our glory, so that He can receive all the glory.

He teaches us to focus on Him and there in His presence alone we start to see our Divine Life path. This path is filled with love, Divine Life, and an ever flowing river, a fountain that we can drink from and never thirst again. With His love in us, we are able to have fellowship with Him. Words cannot describe my closeness to Yeshua, it is called the fellowship of His sufferings, which leads me into such   a close relationship, fellowship and union with Him.

Reflection:
- YHVH invites you to come and drink from His Fountain of Life.
- He wants you to bask in His pure love for you.

Response:
Come and bow in His presence today, laying everything at the feet of Yeshua.

Take up your cross

Then He said to them all, "If anyone desires to come after Me, let him deny himself, and take up his cross daily, and follow Me."
Luke 9:23 [NEW KING JAMES VERSION]

His love triumphs over all suffering and trials, even the greatest pain and death. I realize that I must overcome the deep suffering and pain that I cannot speak about. Each day that I pick up my cross and follow Him I overcome. I understand the fight with pain in your body. I understand the pain of losing a loved one. I understand the pain of brokenness.

But, the pain that keeps me humble is the pain of the careless words that people speak about my child. An example of this is, "I met Aldo, and it was not what I expected, he is still struggling to speak and walk. He could not even communicate with me. I was so disappointed; he could not even give me a Word." Even though I keep on telling the world that Aldo has a brain injury, and he is still broken, they expect perfection? Why? Abba never asks for perfection, but wholeness of heart. Why is it that we are so surprised that YHVH can use the foolish things of the world to teach the wise? Why do you think, his letters are so filled with Wisdom, but still you expect him to be perfect? I look at his brokenness and see an even bigger miracle.

Reflection:
* There are many different types of pain that people have to bear. What is your pain?
* Are you overcoming in the Name of Yeshua? The way to do it is one day at a time.

Response:
Ask Holy Spirit to help you to take up your cross daily and follow Yeshua.

A life changing process

For thus says the High and Lofty One who inhabits eternity, whose name is Holy: "I dwell in the high and holy place, with him who has a contrite and humble spirit, to revive the spirit of the humble, and to revive the heart of the contrite ones."
Isaiah 57:15 [NEW KING JAMES VERSION]

What a journey—walking in absolute dependency on Yeshua! We all walk the Lazarus-journey from death in our spirits to Life in Abundance as YHVH has promised. Step-by-step He brings us back to life, transforming us into His likeness. As the stone was removed from Lazarus' grave, the Light and Truth shone in bringing Life.

This is a LIFE CHANGING process. Because YHVH loves us so much He will not give up on us. Lazarus couldn't hear the people mourning for him at his grave. The saddest part was that he wasn't even aware of Yeshua's presence. That part—the trauma—in all of us, is completely dead! And it is dead because of iniquity, sin, transgressions and pain. This is not physical death, but spiritual death. We all inherited a family occult bank filled with memories that were passed down from parents to children. That bank is under the control of the Baal system and his ways. The broken spirit part (emotion) of a person with all its Baal senses is in the valley of death or hell, covered with grave clothes and shackles. Darkness and lies filled with tormenting are all that he sees and hears. We on the other hand have the choice of hearing and obeying Yeshua's voice as He calls us to come out of the tomb.

Reflection:

- Are you walking in absolute dependency on Yeshua, or are you still closed up in the tomb.
- Like Lazarus we have to heed the call to come out into the Light and Truth.

Response:

Take the first step today. YHVH has promised to revive the spirit of the humble.

His Light shines upon you

The people who walked in darkness have seen a great light; those who dwelt in the land of the shadow of death, upon them a light has shined.
Isaiah 9:2 [NEW KING JAMES VERSION]

People tell me, "My husband, wife, child or parents do not want to hear what I say to them?" They cannot hear you! They are trapped and all their senses are dulled. All you will be able to see is their nature of darkness being fed by death. The stone before the grave needs to be removed so that Life, Love and Light can shine into their darkness! You remove the stone through prayer and by faith breaking all the legal rights that the enemy has to keep them in the grave.

This starts with acknowledging the darkness. Yeshua paid the full price. We don't see with the eyes of understanding (faith) what happened to us in the spirit. So, in order to survive we want to fight in the flesh with our tongues or try to dull the pain with Pharmacia (poisons). Yeshua promised that He will never break a broken reed (Matthew 12:20). The broken reed is a heart that becomes progressively harder. The spirit inside dies over time because of sin and pain. All the anointing of Yeshua's life and destiny in us seeped out and the reed became brittle from years of serving the Baal Sun god in our darkness. The reed needs to be restored. We need our spirit to be healed, cleansed and filled with the anointing of Holy Spirit.

Reflection:
*   Have you got loved ones who are trapped in the darkness?
*   Are you faithfully praying for them, and breaking all the legal rights that the enemy has?

Response:
Always remember that YHVH is all powerful. He has promised you that His Light will shine upon you.

A renewed mind

That you put off, concerning your former conduct, the old man which grows corrupt according to the deceitful lusts, and be renewed in the spirit of your mind, and that you put on the new man which was created according to God, in true righteousness and holiness.

Ephesians 4:22-24 [NEW KING JAMES VERSION]

In the grave you cannot sense the presence of Yeshua, you cannot hear Him, or even see the goodness and kindness that people or YHVH offer you. You cannot respond to the call of Yeshua, and you are not in fellowship with Him. In this place your spirit is not one with His. There is a difference between resuscitation and resurrection. In resuscitation you die again and again, but when the King of Glory comes and resurrects your dead spirit, you are alive forever more. All the darkness in us needs to be resurrected and Lazarus needs to come alive again! And the only way is to take full responsibility for our lives and our actions, to bring everything to Yeshua, to repent and to ask Him to wash us with His Blood.

Through this process I found that there was a much deeper battle, as deep as the seed of man. And this hook that is in man, keeping him in the grave, is the occult seed in him. This hook came about when our forefathers made covenants with death and Sheoll (Isaiah 28:18). Yeshua died to give us Life in abundance. He gives us a renewed mind that can be stable and focused upon Him. We have to make the choice to take the step of faith and come out from the tomb into the Light.

Reflection:
*   Meditate upon everything that YHVH has been saying to you over the past days.
*   Thank Him that He has given you a renewed mind that is stable and focused.

Response:
Recommit yourself to walking by faith in the fullness of what Yeshua has given to you.

*Praise be to the God and Father of our Lord Jesus Christ,
who has blessed us in the heavenly realms
with every spiritual blessing in Christ.
For he chose us in him before the creation of the world
to be holy and blameless in his sight.
In love he predestined us for adoption to sonship
through Jesus Christ, in accordance with his pleasure
and will—to the praise of his glorious grace,
which he has freely given us in the One he loves.*
Ephesians 1:3-6

Finding your
true destiny

'For I know the plans and thoughts that I have for you,'
says the Lord,
'plans for peace and well-being and not for disaster
to give you a future and a hope.'
Jeremiah 29:11 [AMPLIFIED BIBLE]

Living in Yeshua

It is the soul, the natural man that keeps us away from our true identity in Christ. When man sinned, his spirit-man died. He who sins, and keeps on sinning, is no longer spiritually alive. They are insensitive to and unable to discern the things of the Spirit. This is why Yeshua said that in order to see the Kingdom of YHVH a person must be born again. This means that "self" has to die and make room for Holy Spirit. When a person dies physically he is quickly removed from society, from the living and buried amongst the dead in a cemetery. Yeshua taught that the dead cannot stay among the living. When we are dead in our sins, we cannot live and understand the meaning of living in the Spirit.

The person without the Spirit does not accept the things that come from the Spirit of God but considers them foolishness, and cannot understand them because they are discerned only through the Spirit (1 Corinthians 2:14). The Bible speaks clearly about a person who is dead in sin. Sadly, so many Christians find themselves in this state—and do not understand the things of the Spirit of YHVH. Therefore, just as sin entered the world through one man, and death through sin, and in this way death came to all people, because all sinned (Romans 5:12).

Reflection:

- Dead people cannot hear. You need to be spiritually alive in order to hear Yeshua's voice.
- What are you: Dead or alive spiritually?

Response:

How did you answer the question in the Reflection and what do you plan to do about it?

Open or closed ears?

To whom can I speak and give warning? Who will listen to me? Their ears are closed so they cannot hear. The word of the Lord is offensive to them; they find no pleasure in it.
Jeremiah 6:10

The prophet Jeremiah lamented the fact that the peoples' ears were closed and they could not hear the word of the Lord. They found it offensive and they took no pleasure in it. This is in direct contrast to what David wrote: *They are more precious than gold, than much pure gold; they are sweeter than honey, than honey from the honeycomb* (Psalm 19:10). By nature any individual who disobeys Yeshua's voice is a prisoner to the law of sin and death. Self-centeredness and pride are deeply rooted in all of us. These blind us and become part of us, and they form our character. This character is flesh. It reflects the nature of our flesh and not the image and likeness of Yeshua—Christ in us.

Flesh gives birth to flesh, but the Spirit gives birth to spirit (John 3:6). The Word also says that Yeshua is a Life-giving Spirit, and that the Spirit gives Life to us, and that there is life in the blood. Therefore, to be born of the Spirit is to be born of the blood of Yeshua. *For the life of a creature is in the blood, and I have given it to you to make atonement for yourselves on the altar; it is the blood that makes atonement for one's life* (Leviticus 17:11).

Reflection:

- Read Jeremiah 6:10 again. Are your ears closed or open? Do you take pleasure in Yeshua's Word?
- What has Holy Spirit been saying to you today as you read God's Word?

Response:

Write a prayer in response to what Holy Spirit has said to you.

Listen to Him

You have declared this day that the Lord is your God and that you will walk in obedience to him, that you will keep his decrees, commands and laws—that you will listen to him.
Deuteronomy 26:17

When the leper Naaman came to Elisha to be healed, he was told to wash himself seven times in the Jordan River. And when he did this, he was miraculously healed of leprosy. First of all Naaman had to listen to what Elisha said to him. Then he had to choose to obey the command of the Lord spoken through Elisha. Only when he acted in obedience upon what he heard was he healed.

Likewise, we have to hear the Word of Yeshua to us and obey Him by washing ourselves in Yeshua's blood. When we do this we will experience the death of our old self and we will receive new Life in Christ Jesus. Those who die to sin and choose to live in the Light of Christ, in His righteousness, will experience a new Life. This new Life that we receive from Yeshua means that we live in a new way. When we die to self and are raised up in Him the old passes away and everything becomes new. It means that we leave our old ways of pleasing ourselves behind us and we start focusing on Yeshua and His will. We listen to and obey His voice speaking to us. We have the promise that we will become what we gaze upon.

Reflection:

- What or whom are you gazing upon?
- What evidence is there in your life of the new Life that you have in Yeshua?

Response:

Read Deuteronomy 26:17 again and make a declaration of your obedience to YHVH.

A surrendered heart

I have come into my garden, my sister, my spouse.
Song of Solomon 5:1a [NEW KING JAMES VERSION]

Life is a journey. As I look around I see many people who are suffering and in pain. Yet few understand what is really going on in their lives. My family and I are fighting the good fight of faith. This fight forces you to leave everything behind to follow the King—no matter how painful it is. The other option is running after your fleshly, worldly dreams hoping they will bring you comfort and status. I know exactly how it feels when all your dreams are shattered and you are left picking up the broken pieces of your life. When this happens you have a choice. Either you can try to fix it or you surrender it all to Yeshua.

Many years ago I realized that in that humble, totally dependent place there is a garden inside of every man. It is filled with Abba Father's dreams for you. Sadly, most of our gardens are filled with our own desires, dreams, self-worship and extolment. It is there that people live a hidden life, in their inner world. A life filled with secrets and fleshly desires built up out of everything that is not surrendered to Yeshua. This place is filled with self-desire, is always in darkness and brings no life! But, as we lay these down, He replaces them with His dreams of love and peace for you.

Reflection:
- Abba Father can only work in your life when your heart is surrendered to Him.
- Are you trusting Him to make His dreams for you a reality?

Response:
Speak to Holy Spirit about where you find yourself right now in your walk with YHVH.

A perfect Destiny

As God's co-workers we urge you not to receive God's grace in vain.
2 Corinthians 6:1

We all have a perfect Destiny, and a divine spiritual DNA inherited from the Perfect Divine gene pool. This is what brings true change in us. We see this process throughout Scripture: Jacob who turned into Israel; Saul the murderer who changed identity to become Paul—the one who loved Yeshua and took His Gospel to the entire world. This is what we can expect as His children when our DNA changes into His.

But, just like all of us, the Biblical characters also walked around the mountain many times before they made a decision to start climbing their Divine Destiny in Christ. Only after they found their true identity and spiritual DNA, could they start ascending their 'Divine Life's' mountain. Most often it is our circumstances that press us to move into our rightful place in life. We do not need to view our daily walk and current circumstances as negative or difficult. No, if we understand the Father's love for us our focus would shift to the redeeming work He is busy with. I am very sure that if it wasn't for my journey of pain and suffering, I would not be on this mountain today. Even through tears am I thankful that I am saved out of my past life, even if the journey is never smooth sailing.

Reflection:
- Do you believe that you have a perfect Destiny?
- Or do you view your life and what you are experiencing negatively?

Response:
Ask Yeshua to help you to see your life and your circumstances through His eyes.

Overcome the world

For everyone born of God overcomes the world.
This is the victory that has overcome the world, even our faith.
1 John 5:4

Before finding your true identity and YHVH's "Divine Plan" the journey can be very tiring. We need to surrender all to Yeshua. We have to come to a place of knowing Him and accepting His sacrifice, and understanding the depth of it. Then we can take our place in "YHVH's Divine Plan" for our lives. One thing I am very sure of, and that is that His plan is not for us to keep on walking round and round the mountain—getting nowhere. No, we have to start climbing the mountain—step by step, overcoming each obstacle on the way. He wants us to be overcomers.

We need to be willing to accept YHVH's assessment of who we are. So, what is YHVH asking of us? "Are you willing My child, to let go of the name Simon Bar–Jonah and become Peter? Are you? Are you willing to let go of your past?" Our divine spiritual DNA was engineered to supersede the circumstances of our natural life. I have in my spirit all that I need to overcome every mountain and obstacle in my life. I have all the revelation, truth, gifts as well as the Spirit of Life in me, to overrule all darkness and death in me. After letting go of the old Retah, I could start climbing my "divine spiritual mountain."

Reflection:
* What are the steps to finding YHVH's "Divine Plan" for your life?
* Are you wasting energy walking around and around the mountain?

Response:
The first step is surrender—have you taken it?

Climbing the mountain

In him was life, and that life was the light of all mankind.
The light shines in the darkness, and the darkness has not overcome it.
John 1:4-5

My bloodline identity is being changed for eternity. I have taken full responsibility for my mistakes, my past, and my evil DNA. This means that step by step I am trading; the darkness for Light; lies for the Truth; a double life for a Life in Christ, and a double mind for the Mind of Christ. Once I have dealt with my old ways, my flesh, and my DNA through repentance and the Blood of Yeshua I can say that I have been redeemed and regenerated. I can know who I am in Christ. The "old" Retah is dead and buried. The real me, created in His image and likeness needs to be awoken to take up the responsibility for my future. Then I can start to climb my mountain, moving into my perfect Destiny that YHVH has for me. No more trips around the mountain.

People say, "I need to find myself." But, all you need is to find is Yeshua and your spiritual DNA. Once Peter recognized the divinity of Yeshua, he found himself. He wasn't perfect from that moment on. The man Yeshua called "the rock" still denied Yeshua three times. Yet, as far as YHVH was concerned, Peter would always be "the rock." Peter's life, like ours, was not connected to self, but to every Word that proceeds from the mouth of YHVH.

Reflection:

- Have you got to the place where you are able to take full responsibility for your past?
- Is the "old" .... dead and buried?

Response:

What do you have to do to begin moving into the fullness of what Yeshua is offering you?

Come to YHVH

"Come to me, all you who are weary and burdened, and I will give you rest. Take my yoke upon you and learn from me, for I am gentle and humble in heart, and you will find rest for your souls. For my yoke is easy and my burden is light."
Matthew 11:28-30

Yeshua called Peter and he came (Matthew 14:29). He believed that he could do the impossible. Our destinies are not connected to self, but to what YHVH says! So, you can trade the chaos of your life for order, and the darkness for Light because your life is stamped with your new DNA. How the enemy hates this Heavenly trading! But, why are people so afraid to trade the old for the new and the known for the unknown? The enemy keeps on whispering into our ears, "You will never get out of this chaotic life and this evil DNA, you won't amount to anything." But Yeshua says, "Come to Me. I will take you higher than you could ever go, just come. Step by step I will take you out; it is all inside of you. The weaker your flesh, the stronger your spirit is. Come! Climb with Me."

It doesn't matter what you come out of, or that you have to start at the bottom. Ruth came out of Moab. I came out of an evil DNA. Yet when we respond to His call to "come" we will all rise far above our origins or circumstances. I read in the Word that Ruth's losses were reversed, her reputation was restored and she accomplished great things for YHVH. But you have to respond to His call and "come!"

Reflection:
- Your Destiny is to walk with YHVH in His Light and Life.
- What is it that you will have to leave behind in order to heed YHVH's call to "come?"

Response:
Tell YHVH that you will gladly respond to His call on your life.

Pressing on

Not that I have already obtained all this, or have already arrived at my goal,
but I press on to take hold of that for which Christ Jesus took hold of me.
Philippians 3:12

The TRUTH is the substance of life, and not just mere knowledge. The TRUTH shall set you free, and shall give you rest—also within yourself. Yeshua wants to take your hand on the journey of climbing your spiritual mountain. It is done out of a place of rest, of dying to self. He wants us to walk in His ways—the Divine Destiny that YHVH has prepared for us before the foundation of the world—that He has already imparted into our spirits. All that we need for this journey is already in our spirits, unpacking it step by step as we die to self.

In Yeshua's Kingdom we grow step by step, it is not given to you on a platter because of who you are. We all have to climb the mountain; there is no quick way. And in the climbing the dying to self happens with the goal being total dependency on YHVH. It is like the mantel I saw in the spirit. It was so beautiful, beaded with Sapphires and gemstones, but the only problem with it was that it was so tiny. Holy Spirit softly said to me "don't worry, the more you grow in dying to self, the sooner it will fit you. You will grow into the mantel by dying to self, Retah."

Reflection:
*   The only way to be able to reach and walk in your Divine Destiny is to die to self.
*   How are you doing as you climb your mountain?

Response:
Commit yourself to the process of climbing your mountain.

Take YHVH's hand

So do not fear, for I am with you; do not be dismayed, for I am your God. I will strengthen you and help you; I will uphold you with my righteous right hand.
Isaiah 41:10

Fear opens the door to captivity in our lives. This is why going through a trauma opens so many doors for the enemy. But the cure for fear is faith that comes from the Word of YHVH. Stand on the Word of YHVH and His promises. Fill your mind with His Light and Truth. Uproot the works of Satan in your life. Don't listen to words of fear, but listen to the Word of YHVH.

Faith is to keep on trusting Yeshua without knowing the answers. Faith is trusting Yeshua that He will take my pain and turn it around for His Glory. Faith is to trust Yeshua that He will use all my brokenness and transform me into His image and take me into my Divine Destiny in Christ. Faith is to embrace the truth about Yeshua and myself, and to let go of the enemy's lies. You can run but you cannot hide. Yeshua knows everything about you so open up your pain to His love. *"Am I a God near at hand,"* says the Lord, *"And not a God afar off? Can anyone hide himself in secret places, so I shall not see him?"* says the Lord; *"Do I not fill heaven and earth?"* says the Lord (Jeremiah 23:23-24). So take His hand so that He can lead you out of fear into Truth.

Reflection:
- Fear will prevent you from entering into your Divine Destiny.
- Are you trusting Yeshua even though you do not have all the answers right now?

Response:
Tell YHVH that you want to take His hand so that He can lead you.

Truth brings freedom

*For those God foreknew he also predestined to be conformed to the image of his Son,
that he might be the firstborn among many brothers and sisters.*
Romans 8:29

All of us, no matter who we are, know brokenness—but, I ask you to choose Life and His Light. The love of YHVH has a life changing ability. Physical healing will be the result as His love reaches into the depths of your soul. Yeshua wants to use us all as vessels of honor to channel His Love. Every weekend as I minister I see that His love brings healing, His Grace opens up eyes to expose the lies that are believed; and Truth brings freedom to people. In true love there will be truth. In conditional love there will be lies and masks to hide our deep pain. It is mostly because of fear that people don't want to come into the Light and acknowledge the true condition of their souls.

What a pity that parents don't understand that they are their children's gate keepers. What you hold onto in secret will be passed on to your children in the spirit. This is sooooooo true! Unless we know the healing power of His Love our personalities can never reach the height of usefulness that YHVH has intended for us. Have you reached that place—that Divine Destiny in Christ—there in His heart in the Holy of Holies?

Reflection:
- You cannot help your brokenness, but you can control what you do about it.
- Healing will only come when you surrender to YHVH in everything.

Response:
Have you come to the place of surrender or are you still struggling to do it?

Entering the Promised Land

"Now then," said Joshua, "throw away the foreign gods that are among you and yield your hearts to the Lord, the God of Israel." And the people said to Joshua, "We will serve the Lord our God and obey him."

Joshua 24:23-24

I believe with all of my heart that it is YHVH's heart for His children to enter the Promised Land. But we need to make the choice to enter our Destiny. YHVH wants us to live in and from His heart. He wants us to come into the fullness of His plan for our lives. This is the place where the sons of YHVH will be manifested. They will be those walking in total transparency—overcomers of the evil seed inside of them. They will possess the Promised Land step-by-step as they break all the evil covenants made by them and their forefathers and they will walk in the fullness of their Covenant Love relationship with Yeshua.

Yeshua has a perfect Divine Destiny for every individual's life. But, we need to return to Him, we each need to take back the land, our purpose and the calling for our lives. Yes, the Word says that it will be war; a journey filled with trials and tribulations. We will find ourselves in conflicts and battles. But, the battles are all to claim back the land that was promised to our forefathers. YHVH took man and commanded him to tend, guard and keep the garden from outside influences; as well as not to eat from the tree of knowledge.

Reflection:

- Obedience is the key to unlocking your Destiny and entering the Promised Land.
- Are you going to allow sin to keep you from the Abundant Life that YHVH has planned for you?

Response:

Thank YHVH for the perfect Divine Destiny that He has planned for you.

Self—enemy of your Destiny

The Lord God took the man and put him in the Garden of Eden to work it and take care of it. And the Lord God commanded the man, "You are free to eat from any tree in the garden; but you must not eat from the tree of the knowledge of good and evil, for when you eat from it you will certainly die."
Genesis 2:15-17

When "self" comes in, it opens the door for the demonic and idols to come in. *Little children, keep yourselves from idols (false gods)—[from anything and everything that would occupy the place in your heart due to God, from any sort of substitute for Him that would take first place in your life]. Amen (so let it be)* (1 John 5:21 AMPLIFIED BIBLE CLASSIC EDITION). These idols are anything and everything that takes preference above YHVH in your life. It is that which gives you and your life meaning, identity and definition—this can be your children, wealth, sport, image, religion, friends, job, title and so much more.

Warfare started in the Garden of Eden. YHVH's command was to protect the garden, and to possess the land. In order to do this our body, soul and spirit must be lined up with YHVH's Word. Only with Yeshua as our source will we walk this journey in victory and overcome the giants. It is very costly for man to give up relying on his own flesh. The moment when we enter into the Holy of Holies, into Yeshua's presence all flesh must die. All your man-made ideas of spiritual excitement, great big deliverance or just a new move of the Spirit, or your needs, your ways, your ideas will fade away.

Reflection:
- Read 1 John 5:21 again—what is Holy Spirit saying to you?
- How are you doing in protecting the garden and entering the Promised Land?

Response:
Pray asking Holy Spirit to help you not to allow anything to detract you from moving in your Divine Destiny.

Yeshua, our Promised Possession

"I am with you and will watch over you wherever you go, and I will bring you back to this land. I will not leave you until I have done what I have promised you."
Genesis 28:15

In the Holy of Holies Yeshua is all you want. He becomes the air that you breathe. He gives you direction and strategy, whispers in your ear and tells you what lies ahead of you. There, He shows you the next giant to be faced. He prepares your spirit for war, trains your hands for battle. Replaces your heart of stone with a heart of flesh. The day when you lay yourself down you will never want to return to the wilderness of self-sufficiency, man's opinion, people's blessings or man-made ways, ever again. No one, but Yeshua will satisfy your spirit.

I look at Abraham's relationship with YHVH, and see that he was called a friend of YHVH. A friend who gave his heart to YHVH; and we can see that YHVH shared His heart with Abraham. He showed Abraham great things to come, including all the nations that would come forth from his seed. This Promised Land is Yeshua, our Promised Possession. I AM is the One who will walk before us into the land that He has prepared for us. It is Yeshua who will bring down the principalities and powers, the giants in the Promised Land. It is all through the Cross and His blood that we will be able to overcome the darkness and inherit the Promised Land.

Reflection:
- When last have you spent time with Yeshua in the Holy of Holies?
- Walking in your true Destiny and reaching the Promised Land is dependent upon you dying to self.

Response:
Speak to YHVH about where you find yourself right now.
The only acceptable response is dying to self.

No other gods

*"I am the Lord your God, who brought you out of Egypt,
out of the land of slavery. You shall have no other gods before me."*
Exodus 20:2-3

Mankind has made many other covenants. Isaiah chapter 28 tells of the covenant with death and hell. *Because you have said, "We have made a covenant with death, and with Sheol (the place of the dead) we have made an agreement, when the overwhelming scourge passes by, it will not reach us, for we have made lies our refuge and we have concealed ourselves in deception." Therefore the Lord God says this, "Listen carefully, I am laying in Zion a Stone, a tested Stone, a precious Cornerstone for the [secure] foundation, firmly placed. He who believes [who trusts in, relies on, and adheres to that Stone] will not be disturbed or give way [in sudden panic]. "I will make justice the measuring line and righteousness the mason's level; then hail will sweep away the refuge of lies and waters will flood over the secret [hiding] place. "Your covenant with death will be annulled, and your agreement with Sheol (the place of the dead) will not stand; when the overwhelming scourge passes through, then you will become its trampling ground* (Vs. 15-18 AMPLIFIED BIBLE).

A covenant stands until it is annulled. Because of the evil covenants and agreements still influencing our lives we struggle to enter into Yeshua's fullness. To possess the land we need to break these evil covenants and make a Covenant with YHVH.

Reflection:
- Are you still in bondage to the covenants made by your forefathers or maybe by yourself?
- You will never enter into your true Destiny until the evil covenants are annulled.

Response:
Break the evil covenants and make a new Covenant with YHVH.

Expressing your identity

"Yet a time is coming and has now come when the true worshipers will worship the Father in the Spirit and in truth, for they are the kind of worshipers the Father seeks."
John 4:23

We have to ask ourselves what the source of our identity is. These famous words are so true: You make a living by what you earn, but you make a life by what you give. Things cannot provide you with a lasting identity. Only Yeshua can do this. When your identity is grounded in Him nothing will be able to shake you. To "give" is to worship YHVH. To "stand" is to worship YHVH. To "honor and respect people" is to worship YHVH. To "love unconditionally" is to worship YHVH. To "work out problems with the nature of Yeshua" is to worship YHVH. To "take full responsibility for my life" is to worship YHVH. To "live by faith" is to worship YHVH. To "treat others as you would like to be treated" is to worship YHVH. To "be still" is to worship YHVH.

Do you worship YHVH or do you just live life? I am confronted daily with the reality that we are born to worship YHVH. Only then do you not only live, but you walk in your true identity living an Abundant Life. This worship is part of our everyday life. It does not make you into something supernatural and unreachable. No, in fact to worship YHVH is to be available to everyone. It is to be His hands and His feet.

Reflection:

- What is the focus of your life and what defines your identity?
- Have you ever thought of worship in the way described in the piece you have just read?

Response:

As you spend time with Holy Spirit tell Him what you are going to do about what He has said to you today.

Worship in Spirit and Truth

"God is spirit, and his worshipers must worship in the Spirit and in truth."
John 4:24

YHVH is seeking true worshipers, those who will worship Him in Spirit and in Truth. This is the only kind of worship that is acceptable to the Father. It implies that there is worship that is unacceptable to Him. Any worship that is without faith is unacceptable to Him. In Genesis chapter four we read that Cain brought the wrong offering. In Leviticus chapter ten Nadab and Abihu *offered unauthorized fire before the Lord*. They were out of line with YVHV's prescribed procedure of worship and they died because of it. I see that the same procedure for worshiping YHVH is described in the New Testament. Our worship is required to be Christ-centered or Christ-focused. From this we can see that any worship that is not Christ-centered is considered to be unauthorized fire and it is unacceptable.

I think you may understand it better if I say any worship that comes out of a self-centered motive of the heart is unauthorized. Wherever I travel around the world I am confronted with checking the true motives of my heart. Why am I doing what I do? How do I treat other people? Do I treat them with respect and honor? Do I listen to their side of the story? Do I bring wisdom or is it always only all about me?

Reflection:
- A part of your true identity is the privilege of worshiping YHVH in Spirit and Truth.
- Are you a true worshiper and what are your motives for worshiping YHVH?

Response:
Ask Holy Spirit to show you the motives of your heart and spend some time worshiping YHVH.

Acceptable worship

"Yet a time is coming and has now come when the true worshipers will worship the Father in the Spirit and in truth, for they are the kind of worshipers the Father seeks."
John 4:23

I ask Abba to please teach me to live life, and to worship Him in all I do! "Retah, acceptable worship is My heart for My children. I want you to enjoy our Father-child relationship. My Words, *true worshipers will worship the Father*, means to have an intimate love relationship with Me as Abba." That in itself is a privileged position that we have. But, do you live in it, is it a reality in your life, and do you enjoy it? To be in this relationship of love is worship to the Father. Every day I look out for my Abba's favor, His blessing, and His goodness over my life. And I also teach this to my children. Even when I travel I feel people's love as they put their arms around me in pure love from the throne of grace. I can smile and enjoy His love.

Worshiping in spirit and truth became possible for us with the coming of Yeshua and when He sent Holy Spirit. It is important to notice that even "in the spirit" worship is from the heart, it is not merely emotional feelings. It is characterized by our actions, our thoughts, our attitudes and the desires of our hearts that have been made alive by the indwelling of Holy Spirit in us. This worshiping is a lifestyle.

Reflection:
* Abba Father wants you to live your life in the fullness of His love for you.
* Are you enjoying life as you worship Him with all of your heart?

Response:
Thank YHVH for His wonderful love, mercy and grace to you.

Who is man?

When I consider your heavens, the work of your fingers, the moon and the stars, which you have set in place, what is mankind that you are mindful of them, human beings that you care for them?

Psalm 8:3-4

❝Who" has to do with our identity, and "what" has to do with our Destiny. I read in YHVH's Word that through the Spirit, Word and Blood, we become like Christ— spiritual sons of YHVH. This is the "who"—our true identity. The Cross is not only about "who" we are, but also about the "what" our ultimate purpose and Destiny is. Yes, the Promised Land needs to be possessed, but we do this as carriers of YHVH's nature. That is why YHVH sent Yeshua to reshape us to carry His image and likeness, to become spiritual sons of YHVH. Yeshua consecrates man through His Blood to become a vessel for YHVH. To be a vessel we need to be reshaped by the hands of YHVH. We do not always believe that we need reshaping. Some people think they are complete and perfect after they have been reborn.

In Genesis 1:26a, we find the original pattern and substance of the "treasure" that YHVH has imprinted deep within our DNA. And YHVH said *...Let Us make man into Our image, after Our likeness [meaning resemblance, character]* [AMPLIFIED BIBLE]. So YHVH, engraved or imprinted His character, traits, qualities and attributes when He shaped man's spirit. Let "Us," refers to Father, Son, and Holy Spirit. Then He made a three part being— body, soul and spirit.

Reflection:

- Only in YHVH do we find our true identity and Destiny.
- Are you still looking in other places to find "yourself" or have you fully surrendered to Father, Son and Holy Spirit?

Response:

Write a prayer to YHVH, Yeshua and Holy Spirit expressing your love and gratitude.

Truth

"God is spirit, and his worshipers must worship in the Spirit and in truth."
John 4:24

The Gospel of Yeshua starts with the Cross. There are things hidden in you through the generational issues of iniquity that have been passed to you through your ancestors. It is only when you open this realm of your life, the iniquities in your generations, to the Blood of Yeshua, that His freedom and the Redemption of the Cross will become truly yours. This freedom and Truth is so far reaching and deep that you will experience and know that you are being restored and are becoming one with your Eternal Father. These Truths will enable you in the reality of the Spirit to become who you were designed to be—a supernatural, spiritual son of YHVH.

So what happened? Sin entered through the iniquitous heart of the Serpent. He stole what is of great value, and replaced it very skillfully with a copy. And this is what happened at the Tree of Knowledge of Good and Evil. Man's disobedience/sin allowed the Serpent to switch YHVH's image and likeness within the human identity with his, the Serpent's identity code. This is where sorcery, divination, witchcraft and the evil nature came into all of us—man trying to be like god. When we do this we fall into the deep pit of self-centeredness and become our own gods.

Reflection:
- Yeshua died so that you can be restored and become one with your Eternal Father.
- Are you experiencing this oneness in your life right now?

Response:
Ask Holy Spirit to show you where you are swopping your true identity for a lie.

Our responsibility

So it is written: "The first man Adam became a living being";
the last Adam, a life-giving spirit.
1 Corinthians 15:45

DNA memory is passed on from generation to generation through the Y-chromosome of our fathers and grandfathers, and through the DNA of our mothers. The fact is clear, my DNA is like a memory bank of the history and experiences of my bloodline—good and bad—and it has a direct bearing on the quality of my life today. Even trauma memories are handed down from one generation to another through our DNA memory banks. I look at Paul and see how he understood the power of the DNA's long term memory. *But I discern in my bodily members (in the sensitive appetites and wills of the flesh) a different law (rule of action) at war against the law of my mind (my reason) and making me a prisoner of the law of sin that dwells in my bodily organs (in the sensitive appetites and wills of the flesh)* (Romans 7:23 AMPLIFIED BIBLE CLASSIC EDITION).

He is talking about the unseen law of the DNA's long term memory where the enemy has carried out his scheme to switch our identities and destinies. When Adam obeyed Satan, and ate of the fruit with Satan's DNA hidden in the Word-seeds, Satan was able to write upon Adam's spiritual DNA inserting into Adam's spiritual heart his own perverted nature and character that is the substance of all iniquity.

Reflection:
- It is important for future generations of your family that you deal with your DNA.
- Do you have a deep longing to find and live in your true identity and Destiny?

Response:
Pour out the desires of your heart to YHVH today.

Lack of knowledge no excuse

Teach me knowledge and good judgment, for I trust your commands.
Psalm 119:66

My people are destroyed for lack of knowledge; because you [the priestly nation] have rejected knowledge, I will also reject you that you shall be no priest to Me; seeing you have forgotten the law of your God, I will also forget your children (Hosea 4:6 AMPLIFIED BIBLE CLASSIC EDITION). *Now the doings (practices) of the flesh are clear (obvious): they are immorality, impurity, indecency, idolatry, sorcery, enmity, strife, jealousy, anger (ill temper), selfishness, divisions (dissensions), party spirit (factions, sects with peculiar opinions, heresies), envy, drunkenness, carousing, and the like. I warn you beforehand, just as I did previously, that those who do such things shall not inherit the kingdom of God (Galatians 5:19-21 AMPC).*

A large amount of historical data is recorded within our DNA memories that we have no knowledge of, yet we just live from it. The place of the removal and exchange of our DNA's iniquity is the Blood of Yeshua, the Life DNA of Yeshua. The 666 code in our DNA gives legal habitation to the enemy. It creates a pathway allowing these spiritual forces to legally link into the human spirit and biological framework to do their works hidden deep within us. They influence values, beliefs, decisions and override what is right with thoughts of fear or rejection. This is called the DNA nature, character and behavior of Satan in our DNA.

Reflection:
- We know the Truth so we cannot use lack of knowledge as an excuse for not obeying YHVH.
- You have to deal with the evil in your DNA. For the sake of those you love don't deny or delay.

Response:
Ask YHVH's forgiveness for the delaying tactics and the denial regarding the state of your DNA.

Destined to win

*If we confess our sins, He is faithful and just
to forgive us our sins and to cleanse us from all unrighteousness.*
1 John 1:9 [NEW KING JAMES VERSION]

When I confess my sins redemption begins: The emptying of my human personality, the removal of all pride, and my tainted DNA history. Then the place of being like Adam before the fall can be restored. This is the place where the sons of YHVH will manifest His glory, once again carrying His image and likeness. We will live a transparent life, and we will be reconciled into a love relationship with Yeshua. This is truly possessing the Land. The seven nations had to be utterly destroyed, and not all at once said YHVH in Exodus chapter 23. He said this was to be done step by step! So, the fact that I am born again, does not mean that all enemies are automatically banished from the land!!! No, it means I am called to battle and am destined to win.

When Holy Spirit shines the Glory Light of YHVH upon the written Word it becomes the spiritual "Rhema." This Word produces spiritual faith in YHVH. You receive eyes of understanding. Without these eyes, you will see everything in the flesh! In the restoration process, through the help of Holy Spirit, we will become code-breakers. Spiritual breath will be restored into us, and we will be spiritual sons through The Blood of Yeshua, capable of breathing and living in the realm of the spirit!!!!!!

Reflection:
- You are called to battle and you are destined to win!
- Are you living in your true Destiny as an overcomer or cowering in the corner hiding?

Response:
Ask Holy Spirit to give you a true understanding of who you are in Yeshua so that you can stand tall.

Your inheritance

*I pray that the eyes of your heart may be enlightened in order that you may know the hope
to which he has called you, the riches of his glorious inheritance in his holy people.*
Ephesians 1:18

The Spirit of Wisdom and Revelation provides us with three blessings that would help
us to walk in the full measure of Christ. The eyes of our hearts will then be flooded
with Light, Faith and Understanding. These blessings are that we may know what
the hope of His calling is; what the riches of the glory of His inheritance are; and what the
surpassing greatness of His power towards us who believe is.

Eye has not seen, ear has not heard nor has it entered into the heart of man all the great
blessings Yeshua has provided for us. I know this, I speak this over me and my family, and
this will be our portion! If you are called and set apart, I want you to know that it has been
granted to you to know the mysteries of the Kingdom of YHVH. The Spirit of Wisdom and
Understanding provides us with His "glorious inheritance"—to be whole and free in Christ.
You can choose: Do you still want to hold on to your spiritual inheritance (spiritual DNA) from
your forefathers, or do you want to take hold of your glorious inheritance
from your Abba Father? I am so very excited to declare today that YHVH is truly no man
that He would lie.

Reflection:

- Your true Destiny is not to walk in the DNA of your forefathers, but to walk in victory
  in Yeshua.
- YHVH will not let you down, what He has promised He will delivery.

Response:

If you believe and trust that YHVH will honor His promises to you spend time praising Him
for His faithfulness.

Love YHVH wholeheartedly

"So on that day Moses swore to me, 'The land on which your feet have walked will be your inheritance and that of your children forever, because you have followed the Lord my God wholeheartedly.'"

Joshua 14:9

YHVH will finish what He started in us! I know all that He showed me many years ago will happen because He is God. He waited for us to clean ourselves, to give all our pain to Him so that He can make us whole—becoming a holy vessel unto Him. And I said to them, "You are holy to the Lord" (Ezra 8:28a) [NEW KING JAMES VERSION]. We cannot be used for His purposes if we are not changed into His likeness. And for that to happen, I have to understand what I am fighting. How does it work? How do I overcome? I need to seek and know the Truth. What YHVH started, He will finish! Run the race of faith, and ask YHVH for His Wisdom and understanding.

I constantly have to make choices, and my greatest choice is to love YHVH with all my heart, all my soul and with everything in me. *And you shall love the Lord your God with all your [mind and] heart and with your entire being and with all your might* (Deuteronomy 6:5) [AMPLIFIED BIBLE CLASSIC EDITION]. And out of that place only streams of living water can flow. I bless you with peace to face your giants in you through Wisdom and Understanding. I bless you to be in peace and love and in rest no matter how difficult your situations are. Yeshua is alive!

Reflection:

- What have you learnt about your true Destiny, and are you closer to YHVH than you were?
- If you are still struggling, ask yourself why? What is causing the blockage in your life?

Response:

Tell YHVH in your own words that you love Him with all of your mind, heart and soul.

Then I heard a loud voice in heaven say:
"Now have come the salvation and the power
and the kingdom of our God,
and the authority of his Messiah.
For the accuser of our brothers and sisters,
who accuses them before our God day and night,
has been hurled down."
Revelation 12:10

Kingdom Living

"I will give you the keys of the kingdom of heaven;
whatever you bind on earth will be bound in heaven,
and whatever you loose on earth will be loosed in heaven."
Matthew 16:19

Kingdom keys

He told them, "The secret of the kingdom of God has been given to you.
But to those on the outside everything is said in parables."
Mark 4:11

The keys of the Kingdom are ours; we just need to use them to open the Kingdom over each and every situation in our lives. In my hand, today, I am holding a beautiful golden key that unlocks the vast storehouse of YHVH—it is called "complete humility." This key constantly reminds me that physical strength is insufficient. It also reminds me that I can believe with absolute certainty that *I can do all this through him who gives me strength* (Philippians 4:13).

I have learned that I can go out and do anything as long as I am doing it in His strength. I need never be afraid of what is in front of me, for He is my Strength, my Wisdom, my Way and my All! Today I know that as Yeshua leads us step-by-step obedience is so very important. Because if we are not obedient we will miss the next stepping stone. And if we miss one, then all the steps that follow become challenging and stretching. The world calls those big steps "stressful" but, they are in fact stretching our spirit to learn to become more obedient and dependant with every little step that we take. So we need to choose to stay close to Yeshua each step of the way so that we can live in the fullness of His Kingdom life.

Reflection:
- Is something preventing you from using the key to YHVH's storehouse?
- If so, what is it?

Response:
Allow Holy Spirit to show you what is preventing you from taking hold of the keys of YHVH's Kingdom.

Seek His Kingdom

But seek first his kingdom and his righteousness,
and all these things will be given to you as well.
Matthew 6:33

We are greatly affected by, and trained in, the ways of Babylon. If you could only see the truth! Yeshua is saying to you: "Your captivity is over, come out of Babylon my child. It is time for you to fully lay aside the lifestyle and the ways of Babylon. Come and walk in My Kingdom. Give up seeking self-profit (self-seeking)." Only when we, the Bride, are completely faithful to our Husband can the Kingdom of YHVH's lifestyle rule our lives, our churches, and our businesses. Living a lifestyle that tries to integrate these two kingdoms will always bring about disaster such as: Sicknesses, mind-control, double-mindedness, brokenness, pain, unbelief, distrust and fear.

Serve YHVH with a pure heart. Examine your heart and be willing to acknowledge your faults. No matter what happens to you: If you are accepted or rejected as a leader, whether you are popular or unpopular, praised or stoned, it doesn't matter. Let us seek first the Kingdom of YHVH and His righteousness, then everything else will be added to us. One of those things will be hearing Yeshua's voice. Stop judging other people and stop your habit of always wanting to correct them. Instead allow Holy Spirit to reveal to you what is going on in your own heart. May you hear the voice of Holy Spirit today and come out of Babylon!

Reflection:

- Do you spend your time looking at other people and judging them? If so, why?
- What is holding you back from seeking first YHVH's Kingdom? Make a list.

Response:

Bring your list before YHVH and repent, asking Him to cleanse, forgive and restore you.

What would you choose?

By their fruit you will recognize them. Likewise, every good tree bears good fruit, but a bad tree bears bad fruit. A good tree cannot bear bad fruit, and a bad tree cannot bear good fruit.

Matthew 7:16a, 17-18

Do you remember when Aldo turned 21 that he asked people to pray a blessing into his DNA? As I prayed about this Abba instructed me to use the Kingdom keys to open up His will and impart His generational blessings over Aldo. He had fought all the curses, but it was time for him to receive the blessings.

Each of us who are on a journey with YHVH have to become free from the character of generational curses such as pride, anger, jealousy, and envy. If we do not then we will continue to carry the fruit of these curses in our lives. They need to be removed, and the way to do this is through repentance. Because freedom means having the nature and character of Yeshua in us. Don't think that you can hide this evil fruit. It is not possible, everybody around you will recognize it in you. *Ye shall know them by their fruits* (Matthew 7:16a KING JAMES VERSION). The curse first has to be broken before you can receive your blessing. If not then Yeshua's fruit will not be evident in your life. I made a list of areas of blessing that Holy Spirit showed me. I am going to share them with you in the next few pieces. I invite you to pray them over your life.

Reflection:
- If you could choose any gift, what would you choose?
- Are there generational curses blocking you from receiving these blessings from God?

Response:
Pray to YHVH asking Holy Spirit to show you where the blockages are. Write down what He shows you.

Produce Kingdom fruit

"Therefore I tell you that the kingdom of God will
be taken away from you and given to a people who will produce its fruit."
Matthew 21:43

Once you have dealt with your generational curses you are ready to pray God's blessings upon your life. And to explore and take hold of the keys of His Kingdom so that Holy Spirit can produce Kingdom fruit in your life. Bless me with **Godly character**: Humility, faithfulness, obedience, goodness, truthfulness, righteousness, Shalom where no good thing is withheld and love. That I will have **Spiritual discipline** to always make Godly choices in all areas of my life (body, soul, spirit mind, emotion and will). Help me to be obedient in all things. Give me a hunger for Your Word. Let my generations love You Yeshua, and Your commandments.

I pray that streams of Living Water will flow out of my inner being giving me **New Strength** and that people around me will be able to drink and eat of this supernatural impartation. I ask YHVH that You bless me with peace, harmony, joy, health and success in all that You have called me to do for You. I ask Yeshua that You bless me with Your perfect **Protection** over my life: Body, soul and spirit. You are all I need to protect me from all evil. I pray for a fresh anointing of Holy Spirit fire every day. I also pray that I will know the joy of Your presence in my life forever more.

Reflection:

* If you are still dealing with generational curses allow Holy Spirit to continue healing you.
* When you are ready then you can return to these pages to pray these prayers over yourself.

Response:

As you pray these prayers to YHVH be mindful of what He is speaking into your life.

Provision and Generational Blessing

The Lord has established his throne in heaven, and his kingdom rules over all.
Psalm 103:19

Review what you heard from Abba Father and Holy Spirit yesterday. Before you continue spend some time asking Holy Spirit to open your spirit mind, emotions and will to receive from Him. I pray that I will have an experiential knowledge that Abba is a faithful God; **He is my Provider** so that I, nor my family, will lack anything! Never in my life will I need to worry about what I will eat or drink or what I will wear. YHVH is not a man that He can lie, and those who trust Him will never be disappointed! I ask for the blessing of **abundance** so that my cup will run over and I will always be able to bless others and YHVH's Kingdom.

I ask Abba to impart **generational blessings** into my life. Father, You know what I need. I now take the keys of the Kingdom and open up all the wells that have been closed through sin and iniquity. You know, Abba, how I have been walking the journey of cleansing my generational wells. So please Abba, let Your blessings flow into my body, soul and spirit. Yeshua, please bless me with all the riches that my righteous ancestors have stored up. Bless me with Godly healing through the Blood of the Lamb in all areas of my life.

Reflection:
* Think about what it actually means that God's Kingdom rules over all.
* Where are you holding out on allowing YHVH to have complete control in your life?

Response:
Allow Holy Spirit to continue His work as He reveals things to you and cleanses your life.

The Spirit of Wisdom and Revelation

I keep asking that the God of our Lord Jesus Christ, the glorious Father, may give you the Spirit of wisdom and revelation, so that you may know him better. I pray that the eyes of your heart may be enlightened in order that you may know the hope to which he has called you, the riches of his glorious inheritance in his holy people.
Ephesians 1:17-18

These verses tell me it is possible for every Believer to be anointed with the Spirit of Wisdom and Revelation. I look at Aldo with a head injury, struggling to communicate, but having "Wisdom." This is way beyond analyzing a situation or a Scripture and giving a good response. But rather, it is a spiritual endowment that allows a Believer to go deep into the heart of our Abba Father. It enables us to perceive and understand the mysteries of the Kingdom and our rights and authority through redemption. It is to understand what happens to us through the eyes of understanding. It is seeing through those eyes and persevering in life—not only in the flesh, but also in the spirit.

I see the Spirit of Wisdom as a supernatural impartation of the Spirit. He grants us the ability to see and recognize Yeshua through spiritual knowledge and enables us to understand His mysteries, plans and purposes. In Christ there is manifold wisdom and all the hidden secrets of YHVH. Yeshua wants us to know these. This becomes possible through an intimate love relationship with Him, through personal encounters with Him and living with our head on His heart. From this place we will start to understand with our souls the things that are being revealed to us in the Spirit.

Reflection:

- It is given to you as a child of YHVH to understand the mysteries of the Kingdom.
- Are you going deep into the heart of Abba Father so that you can hear His voice in your life?

Response:

Ask YHVH to give you the Spirit of Wisdom and Revelation so that you may understand the things of the Kingdom.

Victory in the Spirit

So I say, walk by the Spirit, and you will not gratify the desires of the flesh.
Galatians 5:16

Yeshua wants us to understand the things of the Spirit, and apply them in our lives, thus bringing His Kingdom to earth. The apostle Paul was anointed and flowed in the Spirit as he constantly opened up the mysteries of the Kingdom to his generation. That is what Yeshua wants from us. We are definitely in the last days. I believe Yeshua is revealing masses of hidden manna and secrets to us because He loves us and He wants us to be prepared. So many people do not even understand the level of brokenness that they live in. They are ignorant of the fact that some of their broken parts (emotions) have accepted Satan and they have given their free will over to Satan to do his works.

Unless you are totally surrendered to Yeshua and you have dealt with all of your pain, Satan can work in and through you. This could be why you are experiencing a struggle inside. We need to know the true state of our hearts. Ask YHVH to give you His Wisdom about what is going on in the Spirit and even in your own spirit. If not, you will always judge everything in the flesh and will not be able to understand what you are really fighting against or how to gain the victory over it.

Reflection:
- You have been given the keys of the Kingdom but are you appropriating them?
- If there is resistance in your spirit towards the things of YVHV you need to look deeply for the reason.

Response:
Ask YHVH to give you His wisdom about what is going on in your spirit.

The bread of His presence

This is the message for the hour that we live in. We need to carefully receive the "full revelation" of Yeshua our Messiah, as revealed by Holy Spirit through the Word of YHVH. I see how we all try to reach that fullness. People are hungrier and thirstier than ever before for YHVH's presence. But all too often they seek His presence in a manmade way. There is only one way to abide in His presence, and that is to eat of Him. Yeshua has delegated "manna" for each generation of His greatness and Truth. He alone is the foundation of   all Wisdom and all Truth.

We must consume His revelation to be molded into His image and bear His attributes. The fire that you find yourself in right now, that is the fire of the molding process. Yeshua is the Word incarnated in the flesh. You have to partake of Him to share in the revelation of YHVH. Much has been written and spoken about the soon-emerging Government of YHVH. Yes, this is governmental design in its purest form. This is what it is going to look like "Christ in us—the hope of glory." We will share in the mind of Christ, providing an expression of His divine attributes, power and authority.

Reflection:
- Are you hungry and thirsty for YHVH's presence?
- How do you go about seeking His presence?

Response:
Tell Yeshua how much you want to be molded into His image and to bear His attributes in your life.

A reverent spirit

It is our time to have our broken hearts healed, so that we can receive the whole counsel of YHVH in order to be presented to Yeshua and enter into the Promised Land. It was sin that kept the Children of Israel from entering the Promised Land after their deliverance from Egypt. It is the double mind of man, the double values, the double life, the double seed inside of us, and the harlot in us that prevents us from experiencing the fullness of Yeshua!

It is so easy to come into the presence of YHVH. You see, He is the Bread of Life, and He freely imparts it to those who come to Him unbridled and hungering for His presence. However, just as the children of Israel could not enter, many people today cannot enter because they are not willing to go through the fire to be purified, or they refuse to lay down the old ways. You will not enter into His presence if you hold on to your old patterns. But when you come to Him with a reverent spirit the fruit of meekness and humbleness will be manifest in your life. Meekness is primarily being teachable and willing to change when we are confronted with issues contrary to the nature of YHVH in us.

Reflection:
- Is your lack of healing holding you back from experiencing the fullness of Yeshua?
- Are you hungry for the Bread of Life?

Response:
Come before YHVH with a reverent spirit allowing Him to minister into your life today.

The image of Christ

"Take my yoke upon you and learn from me,
for I am gentle and humble in heart, and you will find rest for your souls."
Matthew 11:29

Are you willing to be molded into the image of Christ? You will have to be transparent and truthful. Your hardened heart needs to break before you can be taught. Only then can your spirit open up and receive the fullness of YHVH. Until then everything in your life happens out of your soul. Yes, even your relationship with Yeshua. As you surrender all to Him, your heart becomes soft, vulnerable, teachable, transparent, and gentle. Healing will be the result of this. Pure Living Water will flow daily over your broken heart as you kneel before the Throne of Grace. His liquid love will flow over all your wounds and you will be healed.

Our Abba Father wants us to be yoked to Yeshua in nature and in purpose so that we can come before the Father in the same manner as Yeshua—in gentleness, meekness and humility. Soon we will start to experience the manifest presence of YHVH wherever we go. Thank You Abba this is such a precious gift, "rest for our souls." YHVH teaches me not to fall into the tendency of doing something for the sake of doing it, but to stay still and remain in His presence. In that place—in the heart of the Father—is where we see Him at work!

Reflection:

* Are you willing to be molded into the image of Christ?
* When last did you allow yourself to simply be still in YHVH's presence waiting on Him?

Response:

Do it now. Wait on Him in His presence until He speaks into your life.

Cleansed by the Blood

But if we walk in the light, as he is in the light, we have fellowship with
one another, and the blood of Jesus, his Son, purifies us from all sin.
1 John 1:7

I have learnt so much about the power of Yeshua's Blood. I hold tight onto it. It is such a precious gift that He has given to us. The most amazing lesson that I have learned, and experienced is that His Blood carries the ability to re-create. He re-created my DNA. The Blood of Yeshua can repair broken relationships, broken hearts, broken spirits, broken souls, and even broken bodies. It all happens through the process of exchange, the process of trading on the trading floors in the Heavenly Court. The Blood of Yeshua can re-create broken down structures in the soul, it can enter into cracks, renewing and rebuilding it all. His Blood can heal our broken hearts, our minds and make them all new.

We can go into the memory banks of our hearts allowing the Blood of Yeshua to reform and re-create, making it all new. Memories are links in the DNA strand, and are often buried deep because of pain. They are hidden so deep that instead of bringing them to the Light to be washed by Yeshua's Blood; and trading them through His Blood out of darkness into the Light, we hide them. Many dark spirits latch onto these memories. Even our inherited seed memories need to be cleansed and traded for the thoughts of Yeshua.

Reflection:
- Are you hiding your memories or are you systematically allowing Holy Spirit to bring them into the Light?
- If not, what is stopping you?

Response:
Speak to Holy Spirit about where you find yourself in this process.

Finding your true self

The people walking in darkness have seen a great light;
on those living in the land of deep darkness a light has dawned.
Isaiah 9:2

Bringing our memories into the Light is the only way that our DNA can be restored to YHVH's original plan for our lives and beyond. I think it is time to ask Yeshua to clean our spiritual senses so that we can look through the filters of His Blood. Then we will see absolute Truth. As we continually walk in His Blood, we and our Divine Destiny will melt into each other. No lie can live in His Blood, because He is the great I AM, the Truth, the Life and The Way. Yeshua's Blood re-created us through repentance, it strengthens us and prepares us for our Divine Destiny.

We can defeat the enemy's kingdom because there is nothing as powerful as Yeshua's Blood, and nothing can stand against it. This is great news, bringing hope for all who think there is no way out. This is what Yeshua did for me. He knocked on every cell in my body. Every cell in our body has a door, and He wants to invade every cell in us until we are radiant with His Glory. If there is filth, His fire comes down and burns it all away. This is not always an easy process…. But through all the fire, I found my true self (Retah) and became more and more what I was created to be.

Reflection:
* Following on from yesterday have you accepted that your DNA has to be cleansed?
* Do you not long to fulfil your Divine Destiny in YHVH's Kingdom?

Response:
Bring any stumbling blocks that you know of to YHVH asking Him to begin the cleansing process.

The resting place

To whom he said, "This is the resting place, let the weary rest"; and,
"This is the place of repose"— but they would not listen.
Isaiah 28:12

We should desire YHVH's fire more than we desire gold and silver. His refining fire is the most valuable asset we have on this earth because it prepares us for greatness—a life in Him. Don't despise His refining or think that Yeshua has turned away from you. Refining develops purity, and then we can walk in the midst of His Glory and in His pillars of fire. The pillars of fire in His Courts are the seven spirits of Holy Spirit. And once we have walked through these intense fires never leaving His side, we start to walk in the realm of the spirit, and we start to understand what it is to walk in the Spirit. This is how Yeshua brought divine order to my life, my cells, my mind, my memory and my DNA. He started looking through my eyes, hearing through my ears and speaking through my mouth.

The more His Blood fills you, the more Light you will have, and the more Light you have, the more Life you have! This is His communication place, the place of Glory. Where we enter into His rest. He is Light and He is Truth—and when we are in Light and Truth we will find "the Resting Place."

Reflection:

* Have you been resisting YHVH's fire in your life or do you experience it as His love for you?
* It is your Kingdom right to walk in His Rest, His Light and His Truth.

Response:

Read Isaiah 28:12. Are you like the Children of Israel and not listening to what YHVH is offering you?

Choosing to obey YHVH

*"And teaching them to obey everything I have commanded you.
And surely I am with you always, to the very end of the age."*
Matthew 28:20

❝ My child you are My chosen vessel. Do not be filled with the lust of the flesh, and the pride of life. You will find rest IN ME. Be wholesome, simple, authentic and humble. Simplicity and a spirit of humility are what separate you from the deception out there. Pride exalts itself above Yeshua. Humility helps you be of service. And I do not want you to be worshiped, but I want you to serve My people. Will you, ...?

"This is a new season, and if you desire anything ...., desire more of Me! If you long for anything, long for a greater portion righteousness, and My love in you. My love working through you changes situations. Always remember, your miracle's name is Love! I cannot stay in an impure heart, or a heart that harbors evil and anger. Keep on forgiving, keep on laying down your life. Keep on teaching My children how to maintain wholeness, and inner cleansing through confessing, repenting, and the power of My Blood. Remember, the road to holiness is narrow and steep and often lonely. But there is no other road for you. This is the way that I have planned for you; will you keep on walking and always obey My voice?" Yes Abba, I will. Thank You for never leaving me, and never forsaking me.

Reflection:
* Re-read this piece and spend some time praying through it.
* What is your response to what YHVH is asking you to do?

Response:
Fill your name in the blank spaces.

Forgiveness—the Kingdom choice

Even in darkness light dawns for the upright,
for those who are gracious and compassionate and righteous.
Psalm 112:4

We are all in this process, no one is perfect. Remember, nothing but love can conquer our selfishness, envy and pride. I look into Aldo's eyes and see forgiveness. Even though he still fights so many battles with the enemy, he stands secure in Yeshua's love. His battles are hard because he knows exactly who his enemy is and through whom the enemy works. When we face battles we often want to confront those responsible and ask them to deal with their brokenness, because the enemy works through our brokenness, and always uses it to hurt others.

But, now I know that the battle is in the Spirit and people often allow themselves to be an open portal for Satan. They choose to stay in darkness, and selfishness. Satan uses their mixed seed and brokenness. We have the Blood of Yeshua, so we must become whole, rebuilding our walls so that our brokenness can no longer hurt and fight us. The sad thing is that too few people realize the true condition of their hearts, and they actively choose to stay in denial. I was shocked to once again realize that we are recognizable in the spirit by our ranking of good or evil. Our mantle of Light or darkness. This my friend will continue be a constant fight.

Reflection:
* Are there people in your life who are allowing their lives to be used as a portal for Satan?
* How do you handle this: By being defeated or by taking responsibility for your own wholeness?

Response:
Do you need to forgive someone who is being used against you in the spiritual realm?

Work out your Salvation

Therefore, my dear friends, as you have always obeyed—not only in my presence, but now much more in my absence—continue to work out your salvation with fear and trembling.
Philippians 2:12

Working out your salvation with fear and trembling—it is a constant battle till Yeshua returns. But YHVH's love makes the difference. Love is the fire that burns away every difficulty. Yeshua fills us with love as we empty ourselves from the evil of self and pride. Intercession is the hardest and the most important work. We have to intercede for our children, families and ourselves. I cried out to YHVH from this place of intercession after having made so many mistakes in my life—"please, please help me!"

I need the gift of an intercessory spirit, a spirit of prayer and supplication, taking responsibility for my mistakes. I need to become an open portal for YHVH continually interceding and actively battling for the healing of my family (building our walls). It was all accomplished at Calvary, I cannot add anything. But, as a parent I need to be a cleaned out vessel that can intercede and pray for my children and our generations. "Help me Abba, that I will not miss one day of standing in that open portal, being totally dependent upon You alone, praying for our brokenness." Yeshua told me that I must give myself up to this love. The Fruit of the Spirit is Love. It is Love that will flow through you if you give up on "self."

Reflection:

- Being this vessel that we are talking about is hard in that self has to constantly die.
- It is the only way to take hold of the keys of YHVH's Kingdom.

Response:

Are you willing to be an intercessor for your family? Do you have what it takes to love others?

A change of mind

For, "Who has known the mind of the Lord so as to instruct him?"
But we have the mind of Christ.
1 Corinthians 2:16

There is a battle for and in the mind of man. The enemy wants to keep our minds captive and as long as they are captive, we can try all we want, but renewal is impossible. You can read prayers, you can repeat things over and over again, and you can read Scriptures. But no matter how hard and no matter what we try, nothing will change. The truth is that unless we have a change of mind, our problems and failures will keep recurring.

Our problem is that our minds are trapped in darkness where they are constantly being programed with lies. We need to look the pain or lies in the eye and deal with them together with Holy Spirit. I call it "coming into now-consciousness and dealing with the evil fruits of our lives." You simply have to deal with your hurts, your unbelieving heart, your pride, insecurities and all the other nagging things you choose to ignore daily. You have to acknowledge them and invite Holy Spirit into each situation and/or thought. You have to allow YHVH to expose the roots of your pain. Only then will you see the truth and begin acknowledging your hatred, bitterness, or pride. Then you have to repent and choose to come into the Truth. And only the Truth will set you free.

Reflection:
*   Once the Truth has set you free you will be able to live in Kingdom victory.
*   To do this you need the Mind of Christ.

Response:
Ask Holy Spirit to reveal the Mind of Yeshua to you today.

Renewing your mind

Do not conform to the pattern of this world, but be transformed by the renewing of your mind. Then you will be able to test and approve what God's will is—his good, pleasing and perfect will.

Romans 12:2

Daily I have to ask Holy Spirit to help me discern truth from lies. In doing this I renew my mind into a divine mind—the Mind of Christ. The Mind of Christ renews our thinking setting us free from ourselves, other people's opinions of us, and from our circumstances. It also gives us the Godly Wisdom we need to be aware of and discern the deceptions of the enemy. How can we know if our feelings are true or false? The key is His mind in us. YHVH is able to penetrate deep into the dark painful areas of our souls. He exposes and allows us to see the truth so that we can take responsibility, repent, and come to the truth through Holy Spirit.

Many a time these truths are only exposed during the stormy periods of our lives. Healing comes and we are set free from ourselves and our ungodly thoughts. He roots out the deep hidden secrets of doubt and fear and exposes the strongholds of the enemy. Our Abba Father wants us to know the truth in our innermost parts. He wants us free. YHVH says, *"See, today I appoint you over nations and kingdoms to uproot and tear down, to destroy and overthrow, to build and to plant"* (Jeremiah 1:10).

Reflection:
- Your mind is the key to so many things.
- In order to discern truth from lies you need a renewed mind.

Response:
Ask YHVH to renew your mind and to give you the Mind of Yeshua.

Weathering the storms

I believe that YHVH allows us to be broken through the trials and the storms we face in life so that we will be confronted with and face the dark hidden condition of our minds. Only then will we realize that we need a renewing of the mind. I learn from Job (Job 30:22) that YHVH uses storms in our lives to correct us, teach us and then always extend mercy towards us. He said in Job that the storms come from the "south." And "south" is the Hebrew word *cheder* used in the Bible to describe the "hidden chambers" or the "innermost part of our minds." Or in today's terms you can call it the hidden pain in our unconscious and subconscious minds.

It is the deep, dark pain that carries the evil fruit and brings tormenting and storms into our lives. It will remain like this until we start inviting Holy Spirit in, bringing it all to the "now consciousness." As I then apply the Blood of Yeshua to my dark pain and sin, I will start to taste the mercy that Job spoke of. Yes, we all have storms, but these storms come from our deep inward chambers. He allows and uses this out of His love for us, to set us free from Satan's grip over our minds.

Reflection:
* Do you find yourself being tossed about in a storm at the moment?
* How are you handling it?

Response:
Commit yourself to the process that YHVH is busy with in your life. Use the time to draw closer to Him.

The power of the Cross

For the message of the cross is foolishness to those who are perishing,
but to us who are being saved it is the power of God.
1 Corinthians 1:18

The revelation of the Cross delivered me from all the torment and fear that bound my soul for many years. The day I understood the power of the Cross it became an anchor for my faith forever. It is so necessary to understand that the Covenant Yeshua made with YHVH on our behalf is an absolute foundation for us to experience His unconditional love. When Holy Spirit imparts this revelation in your heart, you will never be the same again. He wants you to experience His love and His kindness, His amazing grace for you a sinner. Many times we just want a touch from YHVH, but He gave us so much more. He wants me to be anchored in His unshakable, unfailing love for me. That makes a huge difference in my walk with YHVH.

'Then you will know the truth, and the truth will set you free" (John 8:32). Holy Spirit wants to impart this Truth into our hearts. The day when your spirit receives this revelation of the Cross and Resurrection, and it fills your heart, is the day when your journey to freedom begins. From then on it doesn't matter what your situation is anymore, or what battles you fight in your mind and spirit with condemning thoughts. You know that you have the resources of YHVH's Kingdom at your disposal.

Reflection:

* Do you understand the power of the Cross in your life as a follower of Yeshua?
* If so are you living in the fullness of this Kingdom resource that the Blood Covenant has bought you?

Response:

Thank YHVH for His great Love in sending Yeshua to die for you; and Yeshua for being willing to do it.

Nothing can separate us

For I am convinced that neither death nor life, neither angels nor demons, neither the present nor the future, nor any powers, neither height nor depth, nor anything else in all creation, will be able to separate us from the love of God that is in Christ Jesus our Lord.
Romans 8:38-39

When you stand in the truth of God's love for you then you are anchored in His love forever. We are Blood bought into an eternal Love Covenant, and that means He loves us with an everlasting love. His love will stand forever and will never be withdrawn. The day when we say "Yes" to Yeshua we can know that we never need to doubt His love for us. His love passed every test, even the Cross and that is why we can be so secure in it. In Him we have complete security and freedom to live a Holy Life. As we invite Him into all our brokenness, and we repent, His Blood washes and cleanses us white as snow. Then the freedom comes as He removes the shackles off of our wounds. He will walk the whole journey with us, and help us step by step to freedom.

Yeshua yearns for a Love relationship with us, established through Covenant. Not a relationship where we only need Him, but one where we will love Him with all of our hearts and minds. When we enter into this Covenant, we vow to be faithful, to care, to respect, honor, and obey. But most of all to belong! This gives us so much security, because the world rejects us, but He accepts us.

Reflection:
- If you are looking for unconditional love then look no further than YHVH's love for you.
- He will never leave you nor forsake you no matter what happens.

Response:
How are you going to love YHVH in return—tell Him how much you love Him and Yeshua.

Abundant Life

The thief does not come except to steal, and to kill, and to destroy.
I have come that they may have life, and that they may have it more abundantly.
John 10:10 [NEW KING JAMES VERSION]

YHVH is a covenant keeping God. Everyone who believes in Yeshua receives the gift of Everlasting Life, an Abundant Life in Christ. YHVH is bound in a love agreement with man. We cannot live this life without Him. It is impossible to please YHVH in our own strength. The only way is in living in Yeshua. Trusting in Him alone. I look back at my past and I see a woman who was so desperate, and so broken. I never wanted people to see the real me, because I was afraid of being rejected. I was locked in an invisible prison and could not escape. I worked harder and harder trying to find meaning in my life through a career. This led to greater striving and the more I achieved the more puffed up with "self" I became.

I needed help so desperately. Today I know that YHVH does hear the cry of our hearts. Yes I did cry out. But the day of our accident I desperately cried out, "Help me Abba, help me!" Everything around me shattered, my child was dying, my dreams for Aldo were dying, and I was broken and dying inside. One night on my face in the hospital I had an encounter with Abba Father. He spoke to me and asked me to give Him everything.

Reflection:
- Often it is only at the point of desperation that we are prepared to give YHVH everything.
- Have you reached that point yet?

Response:
Thank Yeshua for the Abundant Life He gives you.

His perfect love

There is no fear in love; but perfect love casts out fear, because fear involves torment. But he who fears has not been made perfect in love.
1 John 4:18 [NEW KING JAMES VERSION]

In the spirit I realized that I had nothing to give YHVH other than my broken messy life, and my broken child. On the trading floor I traded all my brokenness for His Love, for His Life in me. He showed me the Cross, He showed me the veil that was torn, and He invited me in. There I felt in my spirit how my life changed as His liquid love filled my whole being. I was so transparent in His presence and I realized that He knew everything about me. But still I could see how much He loved me—that is called unconditional love!

He poured His mercy and acceptance out on me. The prison doors opened and still do as we invite Him into our broken hearts. He opens our prison doors and sets us free. How I worship Him for His amazing love! Everything in me is so thankful and grateful for the Cross and His Resurrection Power. Today I am anchored in His love through faith. This is a free gift of Love, a gift of Life. Today I know that it has nothing to do with my efforts, because I cannot fix myself. I want to serve the King because I love Him, and more than that because He loves me perfectly.

Reflection:
- What is your testimony of how you came face to face with YHVH's perfect love for you?
- Are you living in the fullness of His unconditional love for you?

Response:
Tell YHVH how grateful you are for His love.
Spend some time praising and worshipping Him.

Opposite of Kingdom living

Do not remember the sins of my youth and my rebellious ways;
according to your love remember me, for you, Lord, are good.
Psalm 25:7

Do not remember the sins of my youth and my rebellious ways; according to your love remember me, for you, Lord, are good. Psalm 25:7

The world says, "Live for self," but Gods Word says, "Die to self." *"Whoever wants to be my disciple must deny themselves and take up their cross and follow me"* (Matthew 16:24). Yeshua described the "dying to self" process as denying yourself. This is not a negative process, although it is very painful at times. *"For whoever wants to save their life will lose it, but whoever loses their life for me will find it"* (Matthew 16:25).

On the road toward dying to self, we become dependent upon YHVH and progressively closer to Him. As we find ourselves and our identities in Him for the first time, we will start bearing living fruit that will be a blessing to others around us. *"Very truly I tell you, unless a kernel of wheat falls to the ground and dies, it remains only a single seed. But if it dies, it produces many seeds"* (John 12:24). I see how self-centeredness, "our wants and our desires," are the battle that we fight. It is our soul's desires against YHVH's desires and perfect will for our lives. I never realized how much I needed YHVH in my life before our accident. My life was full, but still so empty. Probably because of pride we chase after other "lovers" in life, all in an effort to please ourselves—and this is idolatry.

Reflection:

* Kingdom living is the exact opposite of worldly living.
* Where do you place your faith and trust—in yourself or in YHVH's unfailing love for you?

Response:

Has the time not come for you to lay it all on the altar of sacrifice?

Heart, soul and mind

*Jesus replied: "'Love the Lord your God with all your heart
and with all your soul and with all your mind.'"*
Matthew 22:37

I dolatry takes many forms. It can be a relationship that we value more than YHVH: Loving our children, our job, our bodies, or our dreams. The desire for material wealth can be greater than our love for Him. The need to draw attention to ourselves instead of YHVH. The world is full of idols that dethrone YHVH from our hearts. It is 11 years since our accident and I can say that this journey still makes me die to self every day. I look at the simplicity of Aldo's life and I learn to embrace simplicity and child-likeness. "Self" feeds and grows on the grand and the glorious. With that I do not say that our Abba does not want to bless us with beautiful things. No, I am saying that these things should not become our god, and that we need to be content in who we are and very thankful for what we have.

When you die to self you enter a place of peace and humility, where you do not need to feed on the praise of man. You start to live by pure faith in Him alone, and not your abilities. This is such a good place, deep in His heart. It is the place of Kingdom Living where we can know the fullness of what YHVH gives us.

Reflection:
- Do you know the richness of Kingdom Living on a daily basis?
- Or are you driven by your emotions, circumstances and other people?

Response:
Write a prayer to YHVH, Yeshua and Holy Spirit telling them everything that is on your heart right now.

If my people, who are called by my name,
will humble themselves and pray
and seek my face and turn from their wicked ways,
then I will hear from heaven,
and I will forgive their sin and will heal their land.
2 Chronicles 7:14

Walking in Truth and Light

Oh, send out Your light and Your truth!
Let them lead me;
Let them bring me to Your holy hill
and to Your tabernacle.
Psalm 43:3 [NEW KING JAMES VERSION]

Walking in the Light

When Jesus spoke again to the people, he said, "I am the light of the world.
Whoever follows me will never walk in darkness, but will have the light of life."
John 8:12

We deal with sin through repentance, applying the blood of the Lamb, bringing our sin forever into the Light. In the spirit unforgiveness ties you to the person you have not forgiven. This combined darkness pulls you into the pit of bitterness, ending in death and destruction.

Declare over your life, "I am walking in the Light of YHVH, all I do, I do in His Light." There is power in your tongue, use it to declare Truth over your life and that of your loved ones. Bless your spirit man and spirit mind with Scriptures on Light, there is so much power in blessing. Remember light attracts light, and darkness attracts darkness. Broken people attract broken people. Even our thoughts emanate light or darkness according to our spirit. The thoughts of evil spirits who live in you bring darkness into your mind, and then into your behavior. It is through light that every sphere of life is sustained and nourished. In the spirit we all have garments, and the light of these garments emanates from the mind of each spiritual being. So the darker your spirit mind, the darker your garment in the spirit. I think I am beginning to understand what Aldo meant when he said he saw people in grey clothes on the bridge leading into Heaven, and they could not enter in.

Reflection:
- Have you fully accepted Jesus' invitation to follow Him and walk in the Light with Him?
- Which parts of your life are still in the darkness?

Response:
Ask Holy Spirit to show you the dark places so that you can bring them into the Light.

Elohim is Light

In him was life, and that life was the light of all mankind.
The light shines in the darkness, and the darkness has not overcome it.
John 1:4-5

Aldo wrote, "Mom, I see how the Light becomes brighter and brighter in you." And when I did certain things, he wrote, "That was out of the darkness in you, and all pain is in darkness until we invite Yeshua in. Then He can bring healing and restoration through His Light of Truth and Reality." More and more, we as the Body are confronted with the darkness that is still within us. That is why Yeshua is saying to the Harlot bride, "You have mixed seed inside of you, and I am coming for a pure bride! Not for one with a divided heart."

YHVH's heart for us, as His sons, is to walk in His Light, because then no sin, darkness or disease can latch onto us. And from the Scripture (John 1:4) we see that He is Life, and this Life is the Light of man. So the more Light we have, the more Life we will carry within us. But the opposite is also true, the more we seek Life the more His Light shines on us revealing our trespasses and iniquities. Light comes in when I repent and lay down my old life for His Life, His power and His love in me. That is the power of His Spirit that overrules the spirit of darkness in me.

Reflection:
- Which is becoming more evident in your life: The Light or the darkness?
- Yeshua is the Source of our Life and Light. Only He can bring healing and restoration.

Response:
Ask Holy Spirit to work and move in your heart and life, leading you into all Truth.

Resurrection Life

Jesus said to her, "I am the resurrection and the life.
He who believes in Me, though he may die, he shall live."
John 11:25 [NEW KING JAMES VERSION]

Yeshua said that resurrection is not just an event that will take place in the future and that we will have to wait to see happen. No, He said, that HE IS the Resurrection and the Life. Not that He would become it, someday in the future. It is already accomplished! Yeshua made this prophetic revelation before his death and resurrection. Because He lived through the Father, *"As the living Father sent Me, and I live because of the Father, so he who feeds on Me will live because of Me"* (John 6:57 NKJV), He was aware that the life and power of His resurrection was already in Him, and that He WAS what was in Him. Although He had not yet experienced his glorious change from mortal to immortal. He knew that He could call the things that are not seen, as though they already were.

Resurrection is the life of YHVH in man, and is a present day reality. Yeshua, who is the resurrection, is already working within us and making us alive from the inside by Holy Spirit. *"A little while longer and the world will see Me no more, but you will see Me. Because I live, you will live also. At that day you will know that I am in My Father, and you in Me, and I in you"* (John 14:19-20 NKJV).

Reflection:
- You can rejoice in Yeshua your Resurrected Lord and Savior.
- Yeshua's resurrection makes all the difference to the life you live on this earth.

Response:
Thank Yeshua for His Resurrection Life that flows through you.

Changing from glory to glory

Now the Lord is the Spirit, and where the Spirit of the Lord is, there is freedom. And we all, who with unveiled faces contemplate the Lord's glory, are being transformed into his image with ever-increasing glory, which comes from the Lord, who is the Spirit.
2 Corinthians 3:17-18

We are changing from glory to glory. Resurrection is not something that should happen to us—it should be happening in us. It is in our spirit and should be working through our souls and ultimately change our mortal bodies and the way we live. It is a day by day renewal process (2 Corinthians 4:16) and although we must apply it, it comes out of our regenerated spirit. The Life of Yeshua in us, it is the embodiment of all YHVH's promises. All the Treasures and all the Wisdom are hidden in Him. His Life within us, is our hope of glory.

I want to know Christ—yes, to know the power of his resurrection and participation in his sufferings, becoming like him in his death, and so, somehow, attaining to the resurrection from the dead. (Philippians 3:10-11). The prize and the goal Paul was pressing toward was to know the power of Christ' resurrection in his life immediately. He knew the manifestation of Christ' Life in him would qualify him for a first resurrection and cause him to be truly born of YHVH. Having known YHVH's reign in his life, he could be confident of obtaining a final resurrection with those who *...will be priests of God and of Christ and will reign with him for a thousand years* (Revelation 20:6).

Reflection:

* Do you grasp the importance of what it means to share in Yeshua's Resurrection Life?
* Are you experiencing the daily renewal process spoken of in 2 Corinthians chapter four?

Response:

Allow Holy Spirit to awaken your spirit to the glorious reality of Yeshua's Resurrection Life in you.

Obedient to Holy Spirit

But the Advocate, the Holy Spirit, whom the Father will send in my name,
will teach you all things and will remind you of everything I have said to you.
John 14:26

As I was packing before our move to Cape Town I found Rebecca Brown's book. The title of the book is *Unbroken Curses*. I could hear Holy Spirit say to me "take a look at this book." "No, I am so tired of curses, I don't want to read anything further!" "Retah, look at the book!" By then Yeshua had my attention. I sat down and opened the book on page 40. The heading reads, *Breaking dedications to Satan.*

Satan wants the children! Every parent or grandparent who served and worshipped Satan or a demon god of any sort (occult – sangomas, tarot cards, palm reading, racism, money, fame and pacts to ensure success) has dedicated their children and descendants to the service of Satan. You have the beast – Satan's nature, or you have Yeshua's nature. I have found that Lazarus has the beast's nature in him, because he believed the lies; and he was or is in death and hell shackled with these kinds of curses. All these things happen to us, and we stay in the grave and have the Lazarus anointing and nature. That makes us the Harlot bride with the mixed seed in us. He, Lazarus; our wounds with the curses in it are sealed with covenants; and has to be redeemed and brought to the light all through the Blood of Yeshua.

Reflection:
* When Holy Spirit speaks to you do you obey or carry on with your own agenda?
* Is the Lazarus spirit at work in your life and the lives of your family?

Response:
Ask Holy Spirit to show you where you may have let Satan in through the things you have done.

Life and death

This day I call the heavens and the earth as witnesses against you
that I have set before you life and death, blessings and curses.
Now choose life, so that you and your children may live.
Deuteronomy 30:19

We continue reading from Rebecca Brown's book, *Breaking dedications to Satan*. *When a child, or even an unborn offspring is dedicated to the service of Satan (without you even knowing it) demon spirits are assigned the task of injuring that child, and that child remains in the service of Satan all his life. Such dedications may not be worded with these exact words. These dedications, and the implied bondage, are inherited from generation to generation. Once a person who has been dedicated in such a way accepts Yeshua as his Lord and Saviour, he effectively breaks the dedication. To the demon spirits that were assigned to insure his fulfilment of the dedication to Satan, he then becomes a traitor – an ancient human spirit. As retaliation a curse of destruction is immediately launched against the saved person. You see, the demonic philosophy is something like this: if a person can't be held to his dedication, the demons will attempt to destroy him.*

She goes on to explain that in the ritual (sin of choosing another god above YHVH) you give over your free will and your children's free will to Satan, you have sworn allegiance to him forever. What does it look like in our lives? We are being cursed, then he hurts us through trauma and so pain sets in.

Reflection:
* Tragically we often do things without realizing their ramifications.
* This is why it is vital for us to break these curses in our lives.

Response:
Ask Holy Spirit to reveal to you the areas in your life where Satan has a legal foothold.

There is hope

For you have delivered me from death and my feet from stumbling,
that I may walk before God in the light of life.
Psalm 56:13

Satan throws us in the grave and rolls the stone in place. That is the story of any Lazarus out there. Many times it becomes so dark and the tormenting so fierce that these broken parts (emotions) of man, our Lazarus', give in to the demonic and take on the nature of the father of darkness. They accept the inheritance, and live a life of death and destruction, giving in to the maxim, "if you cannot beat them join them." But the good news is that Yeshua loved Lazarus, and He gave His Blood for Lazarus to set him free forever.

Here is how you deal with the curses and dedications to Satan: I would suggest that you go to Court in Heaven and state your case. Take your Lazarus situation to YHVH. He is the Judge of the universe. (On page 149 in *Breaking dedications to Satan*, Rebecca Brown explains how to go to court.) *Confess the sins of your forefathers, ask Yeshua for forgiveness and cleansing. Formally renounce any dedications placed upon your life to the service of Satan, other gods or any of his demons. Renounce all covenants you entered into. Give yourself, and your generations as a living holy sacrifice unto Yeshua. Bind the demons in the name of Yeshua. And ask Him to remove the curse and all evil assignments over your life.*

Reflection:
*   YHVH never leaves us in the dark when it comes to how to deal with Satan?
*   Take heart from the fact that Yeshua loved Lazarus and He loves you too.

Response:
Come before the Court of Heaven and put your case before the Judge of the universe.

Life in Yeshua

"Very truly I tell you, whoever hears my word and believes him who sent me has eternal life and will not be judged but has crossed over from death to life."
John 5:24

find this very interesting because I see so many parents crying out for answers, "Why did this happen?" A new born baby in ICU? And simply because it is easier to say "life happens," we choose the path of least resistance. But I know that is not the truth. My father went to Sangomas because of people who stole from him on the farm. They died, and blood cried out for blood. So we were in an accident, and ever since we have been fighting against an unseen force. This is all so deep, and I do not expect you to believe any of this if your life is perfect. But, I know that I am not the only one who fights this battle.

Yeshua was so good to me; He created "Samuel," an emotional part of Aldo who had a Heavenly encounter. And every day Samuel, through "Holy Spirit Wisdom," writes and teaches me about the battle. The battle is called death and destruction. I think I am starting to understand things better. Lazarus had a battle in him as well; he needed to choose life or death. He needed to get out of the grave and face life. Many people hide in the grave, just because they do not believe that Yeshua came to save them and can unshackle them from these curses.

Reflection:

* Are you evading a situation in your life, choosing rather to label it "life happens?"
* *"...whoever hears my word and believes ...has crossed over from death to life."*

Response:

You choose: Will you believe Yeshua, the Way, the Truth and the Life or Satan, the father of lies?

Take a stand

I receive many emails and as I read them I hear the cries of people's hearts. As I think about them my Bible opens at Paul and Silas' lives. I contemplate what happened to them. I find myself staring into the distance and thinking about what happened to our lives—yours and mine. I think about how for some of us our dreams were shattered, and all we want are answers. I hear how you ask, "Retah, I have done everything I know to do! What now?"

My dear friend, take some time to look at Paul and Silas' life and the choices that they had to make (Acts chapter 16). They could have grumbled and complained or they could praise YHVH. All our grumbling, complaining and feeling sorry for ourselves does not open one prison door. Many times I see how self-pity seals the prison doors even tighter. The more we complain, the more we work for and with Satan, and against YHVH. The more we lose hope the more we hinder Yeshua from working because He needs faith. Demon spirits are always busy and at work, using our words to further chain and bind the situation. We then find our circumstances becoming tougher and more difficult to handle. Someone needs to take a stand. Someone needs to be a Paul and a Silas.

Reflection:

- Do you find yourself slipping into self-pity and asking why?
- What have you learnt from the story of Paul and Silas that is helpful to your situation?

Response:

Repent of your unbelief and ask Holy Spirit to help you to have faith and an attitude of gratitude.

Who will take you captive?

*We demolish arguments and every pretension that sets itself up
against the knowledge of God,
and we take captive every thought to make it obedient to Christ.*
2 Corinthians 10:5

Every time we speak evil about a person, we bind that person in an evil chain of bondage. That person starts to believe all that is being said over him because he is so trapped in that belief system of bondage. *And that they will come to their senses and escape from the trap of the devil, who has taken them captive to do HIS WILL* (2 Timothy 2:26). Our words carry a lot of power and all the negative words that we speak bind our spirits into greater bondage. Sometimes Satan doesn't even need someone else to chain you, he just uses your own tongue together with all your own negative thoughts and fears. Satan's plan is to keep your eyes fixed on the situation you find yourself in and not on YHVH's Word of faith in your heart.

The result of us moving into fear and complaining is that we do Satan's will. We lose control of our senses and we give our wills over to Satan by speaking what he wants us to speak. By doing this we are allowing ourselves to be taken captive by Satan. Then he can do his will and work through us. His goal is to put us and keep us in a place of despair.

Reflection:

- Your actions will determine by whom you are taken captive: Yeshua or Satan?
- Will you come to your senses and escape from the trap of the devil?

Response:

Choose today to take every thought captive and make it obedient to Yeshua.

Choose to praise HIM!

*Praise the Lord. Praise the Lord, my soul. I will praise the Lord all my life;
I will sing praise to my God as long as I live. Do not put your trust in princes,
in human beings, who cannot save.*
Psalm 146:1-3

When Paul and Silas sang praises and their words of faith came against all the negative deeds and atmosphere in the prison. Yes, you could be taken captive by Satan, yes, you could be in a prison, but if you have done everything – then STAND AND START TO PRAISE YHVH. So how do I keep my senses, and my will out of Satan's service? By choosing faith and reliance upon YHVH, choosing praise, choosing to stand, choosing to learn, choosing to be humble, choosing to be in correct standing before YHVH, choosing love, choosing to be cleansed by the Word, choosing to be the least—all so that I can be a vessel of honor sanctified and useful to the Master.

Two forces are at war within us all the time. These are positive and negative, good and evil. Yes, sometimes there are sparks; sometimes there are tears, sometimes there are emotions, sometimes there are no words; sometimes there is only begging; sometimes prayers, but the most power is released out of a place of praise to YHVH. It is from that place where you take your stand and don't even tell the world what you are going through, but focus only on praising His Holy Name. And then once again you realize—it is not about me, but all about You!

Reflection:

- Have you come to realize that much of your disappointment arises from trusting man instead of YHVH?
- When we acknowledge this then the obvious thing to do is to make sure we are trusting YHVH.

Response:

Write a "psalm" to YHVH praising Him and expressing your faith and trust in Him.

Trusting YHVH

But I trust in your unfailing love; my heart rejoices in your salvation.
Psalm 13:5

When Paul and Silas started praising YHVH they showed Satan that they had no fear. They chose to keep on trusting even if they didn't see anything hopeful in their situation. They did not know the outcome, but they knew their God. This is a pattern set by Paul and Silas for you and me. We cannot escape painful and difficult situations, but we can make a choice as to how we are going to handle them. Let's choose today to praise Yeshua for everything. For everything, you may ask: Praising Him even for my pain? Yes, I have learned that praising Him takes my focus completely off of me and puts it on Him. Yeshua is enough for us. Our praise will set others free, as well as ourselves.

Your prison doors will not always open the way you planned them to, or in the time frame you planned. When I started my journey, I cried my heart out. I was telling everyone about my battles. I often felt very sorry for myself. Now more than ten years later I have become quieter. I have learnt to walk my walk, step by step, in faith. These are my circumstances and no one can change them for me. I have to walk them with my hand in Yeshua's hand, my eyes fixed on Him.

Reflection:
* How have you chosen to handle the pain in your life?
* Who do you trust: Your friends, your family or YHVH?

Response:
Ask YHVH to forgive you for your lack of trust. Choose today to praise Him no matter what happens.

My heart trusts in YHVH

The Lord is my strength and my shield; my heart trusts in him,
and he helps me. My heart leaps for joy, and with my song I praise him.
Psalm 28:7

I choose to smile, laugh, and exercise, to stay humble and totally dependent on YHVH. I choose not to look around and be moved by people's opinions. I pray constantly, have a teachable spirit, acknowledge when I am wrong, and most of all I choose to praise YHVH despite what I am going through. As we grow in Christ, our faith grows and we realize that we can only stand if our legs are strong. If we have trained our spirit in Godliness and taken our stand on Yeshua our Rock and sure Foundation!

A brain injury has its own challenges. And I have to run this race with Aldo every day of our lives. But, I made a choice to celebrate life, even in the midst of the storms. Someone commented, "You are moving to Stellenbosch. It experiences a lot of rain and storms." I spontaneously replied, "We are used to rainy days (in the spirit), but we made a choice to rejoice and praise YHVH even in the rain." So often we lose our focus. "Please keep our focus on the greatest event of our lives—the wedding feast—where we will be Your Bride, ready and spotless without mixed seed. These difficulties are nothing compared with being Your Bride. We choose to worship You in Spirit and in Truth, despite our circumstances."

Reflection:
*   Have you chosen a lifestyle where you will trust and praise YHVH no matter what?
*   Or have you chosen to wallow in your circumstances?

Response:
Open your heart, mind, and spirit to the Light and Truth of YHVH's love for you today.

Fight to win

Everyone who competes in the games goes into strict training. They do it to get a crown that will not last, but we do it to get a crown that will last forever. Therefore I do not run like someone running aimlessly; I do not fight like a boxer beating the air.
1 Corinthians 9:25-26

I look at a young man in the Bible named Jeremiah. YHVH called him to be a prophet to the nations. He felt so inadequate because of his age. And this feeling of inadequacy nearly kept him from obeying YHVH's calling and destiny for his life. YHVH called Jeremiah, trained him and then sent him out by His Spirit to faithfully speak His Word regardless of the circumstances.

I look at a young man named Aldo. How the enemy tried so hard to keep him from his calling. But, Yeshua used each spiritual fight in order to train us. YHVH calls you and me in the same way. We are all being trained through the spiritual wars we face. Don't think any fight is in vain. Whatever you give to YHVH He turns around for His glory bringing you out of the darkness and into His glorious Truth and Light. You are fighting because there are things in you (seed) that the enemy has a legal right to. He wants you to become angry with YHVH. But, it is not YHVH's fault, it is the sin in our seed (the weeds) that grow in our lives and this is what we are fighting. It is a walk of "working out your salvation with fear and trembling."

Reflection:
* We are all in a battle whether we like it or not.
* The question is are you battling in your own strength or in Holy Spirit's strength?

Response:
Ask Holy Spirit to empower you and strengthen your arms for the battle.

Reap what you sow

Do not be deceived: God cannot be mocked. A man reaps what he sows.
Galatians 6:7

Everyone reaps what they sow. Satan uses our wounds to keep on hurting us. But, even in this we have choices. When you keep the wound to yourself, Satan can live in the wound (darkness) and continue feeding the wound with the same pain that caused it. If rejection is in the wound, he will keep on feeding your rejection. If sexual immorality is in the wound, he will feed you with lust. When we live in sin, we are separated from YHVH. From this place you hunger and thirst to give other people the same pain.

Or you could bring your wound into the Light, surrendering it to YHVH's healing process, and you will begin hungering and thirsting for right standing with YHVH. Adam and Eve were separated. If you were abandoned, you will have a desire to always abandon others. Out of that wound, fear stands up because we are now separated from YHVH and your spirit can feel it. We were created to be one with YHVH, not to be separated from Him. Fear that is turned outwards becomes "anger" bearing fruits of resentment. And when fear is turned inward it becomes "hurt" bearing fruits of loneliness and sadness. Wounds make us double minded and unstable (James 1:8). Christ wants us single minded having the mind of Christ, a sound mind.

Reflection:

- As you examine your life can you see that you are reaping what you have sown?
- The question is are you going to put a stop to it or are you going to remain in darkness?

Response:

Holy Spirit waits to lead you into YHVH's glorious Truth and Light.

Protect your loved ones

In addition to all this, take up the shield of faith,
with which you can extinguish all the flaming arrows of the evil one.
Ephesians 6:16

We need to recognize the calling on our lives. Jeremiah was already set apart as a prophet in his mother's womb. God has a plan and parents have another plan, and the seed filled with sin in our lives are used for Satan's plan. Which plan are you fulfilling? Start praying for YHVH's plans to prosper in your children's lives. Not your desires, but YHVH's desires. Satan will do anything to keep you and your children out of your callings. Don't let Satan use you to help him accomplish his plans because of your selfish desires. Give your children to YHVH. His ways are not your ways.

I see that God uses Aldo completely differently to the way that I thought He would. He uses him uniquely, through his hand and pen. When Aldo prays for the people at the Spirit School they weep as the anointing touches them without him having the right words, or sometimes no words at all. I stand amazed and see YHVH always has a way where there seems to be no way. Make sure Satan doesn't use you to steal other people's callings. Be careful not to keep them in sin or anger in order to continue feeding your wounds. Love one another enough to walk away from your own selfish desires.

Reflection:
* Are you living in a way that is enabling YHVH's work in the lives of your children?
* Or are you because of your own wounds a stumbling block in their path?

Response:
Allow Holy Spirit to reveal the motives of your heart to you so that you can repent and walk in Truth and Light.

Trained for battle

He trains my hands for battle; my arms can bend a bow of bronze.
You make your saving help my shield, and your right hand sustains me;
your help has made me great.
Psalm 18:34-35

Love lays down everything to do with self, for the sake of YHVH's Kingdom. It is not always easy, because self is so strong. I had to learn to give up "self" and choose God's way, every day, just because of love. Ask Yeshua to open your eyes of understanding and of faith to see the things He wants to show you. Ask Him to reveal you the "weeds" that you are fighting in your seed. Before you can heal you have to first see and then understand your wounds.

Recognize and submit to Yeshua's training. Your spirit needs to be trained to live in Godliness; to come out of darkness into His marvelous Truth, Light and Life. Today, I realize that all the weeds and fighting in the spirit have been my training field. It is there that He trains your hands for war. Learn to listen to Him and to obey His voice. All you need is the hand of Yeshua upon you. The Lord's hand was with them, and a great number of people believed and turned to the Lord (Acts 11:21). His hand is upon you if you are in right standing with Him and choose to obey His voice. YHVH uses ordinary people. Their names are often not even mentioned. But His hand is upon them.

Reflection:
* You cannot be trained for battle in the spiritual realm if you are still holding onto "self."
* Are you prepared to recognize and submit to Yeshua's training?

Response:
Spend some time thinking about your response to the question above.

Remain in Him

*"I am the vine; you are the branches. If you remain in me and I in you,
you will bear much fruit; apart from me you can do nothing."*
John 15:5

It doesn't matter what your history looks like. Yeshua will use you and get you into His perfect destiny. Look at Paul, he persecuted so many Christians before he was stopped by Yeshua on the road to Damascus and converted. That is why he suffered so much afterwards. For again whatsoever a man sows, he shall reap. But still Yeshua's hand was upon him, and He removed the weeds out of him. That was all done as Holy Spirit trained and cleansed him through each suffering.

Maybe your name is not mentioned? I want to tell you today that Yeshua keeps records of everything you do for Him—good and bad. When you repent every bad thing is washed away with the blood of the Lamb. Yeshua's hand is upon you in a mighty way, you just do what you have to do for His Kingdom. Even if the earthly records don't note your name, do whatever you do for the King, knowing that He knows. Remember the most important thing that we have to seek is His hand upon us, being one with Him. Then Yeshua can use us to turn many people towards Him, by Holy Spirit working through us; always with His hand upon you. Even if it is the smallest thing, just obey His voice and be His hands and feet.

Reflection:

- Think about what Yeshua is calling you to do for Him. Great or small it is important to Him.
- Are you faithful in the small as well as the big things? Remain in Him and you will bear much fruit.

Response:

Recommit yourself to fulfilling the purpose that Yeshua has called you to.

Live in the Light of Love

Anyone who loves their brother and sister lives in the light,
and there is nothing in them to make them stumble.
1 John 2:10

We were made to give and receive love, and only love can truly satisfy the heart. It is so easy to find fault where there is no love. When love fills the heart it sees the best in everyone and in every situation. Sometimes the heart of man forsakes YHVH's commandment to love one another. I look at Yeshua's life. He walked among people and He was perfect in every way, yet they found fault in Him. The law that He walked in, was the Law of Love. Love is giving of oneself. Love is living now-conscious; meaning that I do not try to escape my situation, but am willing to deal with it and to face it. Love means being consistently thankful for everything, even if I find myself in a less than perfect situation. Love is content, love is gentle, love is pure, love is kind and not sarcastic, and love is truth!

Whenever we continually find fault in everyone or in every situation that we encounter our minds eat of the forbidden fruit that brings death. Because we can only give what we have inside of us we give death. Our negative words will be the house we live in tomorrow; and our negative words about others will be words of fire against their lives.

Reflection:

- Are you living in the Light of Love? You can only do this if you are dealing with your wounds.
- Take a deep look at what is inside of you—because that is what will come out and touch others.

Response:

Ask YHVH to help you fulfil His commandment to love others.

Draw near to YHVH

*D*raw near to God and He will draw near to you. You see, when we live in YHVH's presence it is not difficult to live in love. When we want His presence desperately, we will desperately draw near to Him. It is the same with our families. If we want our children or our spouse near to our heart, we have to draw near to them. To give love, is to give of yourself.

How do I stay in His love and His presence? In John 7:37 Yeshua says that we should come to Him and drink of His Living Waters. Don't run into the world, but run to Him. Let us determine to teach our children and ourselves not to run away from reality, but to face it and deal with it together. There we will find healing. *I have set the Lord always before me; because He is at my right hand I shall not be moved* (Psalm 16:8 NKJV). We are called to think about Him, to rejoice with Him, to communicate with Him all the time. That is how we stay in Him, and in His love. *My dwelling place will be with them; I will be their God, and they will be my people* (Ezekiel 37:27). What more can we ask than to dwell in Him?

Reflection:

- Is your main goal in life to draw near to YHVH?
- Or do you have many other goals that come before Him?

Response:

As you answer the questions in the Reflection spend time asking Holy Spirit to reveal the truth in your heart.

The tongue

The tongue also is a fire, a world of evil among the parts of the body.
It corrupts the whole body, sets the whole course of one's life on fire,
and is itself set on fire by hell.
James 3:6

The mails that I receive from all over the world are heart-breaking. So many marriages that are broken and the effects of this are seen in the lives of people's children. Broken fathers break their children, and the same goes for mothers. To spend our time obsessing over evil thoughts is not the answer: In fact it is the key to opening up the demonic kingdom over you and your family. Unforgiveness is a breeding ground for greater trouble, for more discontent, and many times ends in divorce.

We need to learn to talk about our hurts and pain. And equally importantly we need to learn to listen to the other person's point of view. To open up our hearts and allow someone else to see all our weaknesses makes us very vulnerable. But I firmly believe in transparency. The enemy cannot come near the Truth and Light, he loves darkness and he uses dark thoughts that become dark attitudes and end up in dark deeds or words. These words come from the enemy's camp, and are fiery darts that kill, steal and destroy. He doesn't need a Satanist to harm our children. He can use broken parents to break them with their tongues that *sets the whole course of one's life on fire, and is itself set on fire by hell.*

Reflection:
* Has Holy Spirit convicted you as you read this?
* Is your home one of Truth, Light and Love or one where darkness reigns?

Response:
Before YHVH commit yourself to spreading Truth, Light and Love through the words that you speak.

Forgive as Yeshua did

Jesus said, "Father, forgive them, for they do not know what they are doing."
And they divided up his clothes by casting lots.
Luke 23:34

Sometimes I can see that people forget the fact that when they married that person they became "one flesh" with them. So if they want to harm her, or him, they are also choosing to hurt themselves. It is like they are counter attacking themselves. "But Retah, I am so angry about what has happened. What should I do because..." You should only do what YHVH says you should do in such situations—forgive one another!

"It was not my fault, and he or she never takes responsibility, it is always me, so how can I forgive yet again?" Through a humble heart, and on your knees. You can ask Holy Spirit's guidance, and you can forgive all the "wrongs," not because the person deserves it, but because you understand that by choosing to forgive you open up the Kingdom over you and your family. I look at Yeshua's life and I learn a great, great lesson, *"Father, forgive them, for they do not know what they are doing."* This is so true because many times people do not know what they do, because they act out of pain or the dark evil in their seed. But we walk in Truth and Light because we are YHVH's children: And we know the value of forgiveness. Because we are forgiven we are free to forgive others.

Reflection:

* If you are hurting because of what your spouse has said or done to you Yeshua understands.
* He is the One who can help you to forgive and walk in Love, Truth and Light.

Response:

Pour out your heart to Yeshua and ask Him to help you to forgive and to love.

Forgiveness is not optional

*"For if you forgive other people when they sin against you,
your heavenly Father will also forgive you. But if you do not forgive others
their sins, your Father will not forgive your sins."*
Matthew 6:14-15

The other day I was confronted with a situation where my flesh was really angry and I thought that I had every right to be furious and not to forgive. But later that morning as I went running in the mountain, I said, "Abba, I choose to forgive that person, and Yeshua, You taught us to forgive those who hurt us." You said, *"For if you forgive other people when they sin against you, your heavenly Father will also forgive you"* (Matthew 6:14). I made a choice to forgive and asked Yeshua to please help me and remove all the memories out of my mind and my heart.

When I got home Aldo said to me, "Thank you for opening up the Kingdom over us by forgiving, if you kept on pondering and did not forgive, you would have opened hell over us." I was amazed! And all the memories just faded and my heart was kept pure. "But Retah, this is not the first time." In Matthew 18:21-22 we read: ...*"Lord, how many times shall I forgive my brother or sister who sins against me? Up to seven times?" Jesus answered, "I tell you, not seven times, but seventy-seven times."* We do not always realize what life is all about. It is not about our spouse and what they do—it is about what we do.

Reflection:
* You hold the key to either the Kingdom or hell being opened over your family.
* Will you allow your stubbornness about forgiving to harm those you love?

Response:
Stay in YHVH's presence until you sort this matter out in your heart—it is Life or death.

Forgive to be forgiven

*"Judge not, and you shall not be judged. Condemn not
and you shall not be condemned. Forgive, and you will be forgiven."*
Luke 6:37 [NEW KING JAMES VERSION]

YHVH is a loving God who uses everything in our lives to test us, to train us and to mold us. As we die to self, we trade all of who we are on the trading floor so that more of Yeshua can enter into us, and we can become a vessel of honor for the Master's use. We need to regularly ask YHVH to give us a "spirit of forgiveness." Some people enjoy carrying hurts and grudges. Those negative emotions will kill you, my friend, if not now, then later! And the sad thing is that we transfer the hate in our DNA to our children, and their children. They inherit the good, the bad and the ugly from us. When we are angry with someone it normally hurts us more than it does them.

Ask Abba to help you to change your old patterns of thinking, and self-sensitivity. It makes me happy to know that He is the *Father of mercies* (2 Corinthians 1:3 NKJV). I love how Peter taught us: *Finally, all of you be of one mind, having compassion for one another; love as brothers, be tenderhearted, be courteous; not returning evil for evil or reviling for reviling, but on the contrary blessing, knowing that you were called to this, that you may inherit a blessing.* (1 Peter 3:8-9 NKJV).

Reflection:
- Are you being eaten up by negative emotions, unforgiveness and bitterness?
- Ask Abba to help you to change your old patterns so that you can come to a place of forgiveness.

Response:
Unforgiveness is serious. Choose not to walk around with this weight slowing you down any longer.

Truth, Light and Life

For "He who would love life and see good days,
let him refrain his tongue from evil, and his lips from speaking deceit."
1 Peter 3:10 [NEW KING JAMES VERSION]

Every day I teach my children to seek peace and to pursue it, because the enemy seeks anger and he pursues it. We cannot be joyful if we carry hurts around inside us. Forgiveness is a daily choice and it tests the condition of our hearts. So make sure you pass the test! The more Yeshua becomes visible in you, the more amazing your marriage will be.

He says to us, "My child, as long as there is divorce in your thoughts, there will be anger and hate in your heart. It is the same with healing, how can I heal your body, if there is sickness in your thoughts? You have to trust Me, that when you surrender your marriage into My hands, I will do the work in your heart. Trust Me and obey My voice. I want your mind rested, and rest comes through faith. Worry is a tool from hell to destroy. Anxiety produces tension. Fear and anger are poisons that kill relationships. You have to invite Me into everything, even into your mind. Remember, whatever you think in your secret thought life, you and your whole family will reap. Make a choice today to sow love, kindness and forgiveness so that you can reap the same. Sow hope, sow faith, sow joy, and sow words of Truth, Light and Life."

Reflection:

* Spend time thinking about everything that YHVH has been saying to you over the past days.
* What are the key lessons He has been teaching you? Have you been obeying His voice?

Response:

Write a prayer to YHVH summing up all that you have in your heart.
Commit yourself to walking in Truth and Light.

*I long to dwell in your tent forever
and take refuge in the shelter of your wings.
For you, God, have heard my vows;
you have given me the heritage of those who fear your name.
Increase the days of the king's life,
his years for many generations.
May he be enthroned in God's presence forever;
appoint your love and faithfulness to protect him.
Then I will ever sing in praise of your name
and fulfill my vows day after day.*
Psalm 61:4-8

Living in YHVH's Presence

For Christ did not enter a sanctuary made with human hands that was only a copy of the true one; he entered heaven itself, now to appear for us in God's presence.
Hebrews 9:24

Thirsty for YHVH's presence

*On the last and greatest day of the festival, Jesus stood and said in a loud voice,
"Let anyone who is thirsty come to me and drink. Whoever believes in me,
as Scripture has said, rivers of living water will flow from within them."*
John 7:37-38

Yeshua promised that the breath of YHVH would satisfy our thirst. He alone can satisfy the deep, deep longing inside of us. *My soul thirsts for God, for the living God. When can I go and meet with God?* (Psalm 42:2). People constantly asks me this question, "But why don't I experience YHVH, or hear His voice, why are my prayers not answered?" Maybe it is because we do not understand Holy Spirit, or because we don't live in the Spirit. We will only hear from Him if we abide in His presence every day of our lives? Often we are living in the flesh, too busy pleasing ourselves and others.

YHVH is Spirit and He wants us to worship Him in Spirit and in Truth. It is there that we will find Him. He is in the Spirit, not in the flesh! Yeshua gave us a promise that His Holy Spirit—His breath would be in us, so that we can experience intimacy with Him and enjoy all He has for us. This is the fullness of life, to be one with Him. Holy Spirit is a Divine gift! It is YHVH's permanent presence with us. *"And I will ask the Father, and he will give you another advocate to help you and be with you forever"* (John 14:16).

Reflection:

* Do you experience YHVH's presence on a daily basis? If not why do you think that is?
* Yeshua promised that ALL who follow Him will know Holy Spirit's constant presence with them.

Response:

Tell YHVH that you are thirsty for His presence in your life today and every day.

Never alone

The Lord replied, "My Presence will go with you, and I will give you rest."
Exodus 33:14

We are never alone if we live in YHVH's presence 24/7. We will be one with Him as long as we walk in dependence upon Him. But the moment we trust in our own efforts and strength to live this life we will experience frustration. The "self—carnal life" is a life lived in the flesh. All the broken pieces of my heart live in the flesh, in self-pity and anger, in unforgiveness and hate, in bitterness, sickness and despair. No prayers are answered in the flesh. Nothing will happen from repentance in the flesh. When we sow in the flesh, we reap in the flesh.

How do I know when I am in the realm of the Spirit? When I cross the line into the spirit, my heart will be transparent and humble; I will have a broken spirit filled with true repentance. I will be washed in the Blood of Yeshua. My sin and iniquities will be traded on the trading floor. I will hear His gentle voice constantly speaking to me. I come and I trade the scar tissue of my soul, also called the "hardness of my heart" for His blood. I become totally dependent upon Him. In His presence is the Glory Light and I am transparent. I hide nothing, taking full responsibility for what I have done.

Reflection:

- Often we want YHVH's presence without surrendering whole heartedly to Him.
- Do you realize that you cannot have it both ways?

Response:

If you are ready for total surrender then tell YHVH right now.

Return to YHVH

In the flesh you cannot see the condition of your heart; but in the presence of His Glory Light you become aware of who you really are. It has always been a humbling place for me. When I go on my knees, the tears just flow. My whole being becomes one with Him. His thoughts become my thoughts, His love for people becomes my love for people, and His grace towards me becomes my grace towards others. So when I have no grace and mercy, then I know that I am operating in the flesh. His presence never leaves us, it is we who choose to leave the Spirit for self.

I gave myself as a living sacrifice to Him, and my whole life became one with His. My body became one with His. Every part of my being magnifies Him. I know that I know that He is with me, so I ask Him about everything and constantly speak to Him. Worship can only happen in the spirit because it is done in union with His Spirit. That is where He shows us hidden secrets, and things that are to come. The scar tissue of our souls blocks His Glory Light and His love. It removes the capacity to love others like ourselves and to live in the fullness of what Yeshua plans for us.

Reflection:
- If His Glory Light has dimmed in your heart it is because you have wandered away from Him.
- What is the condition of your heart: Are you living in the flesh or the Spirit?

Response:
Return to YHVH today and commit yourself to serve only Him.

Draw near to YHVH

Come near to God and he will come near to you.
Wash your hands, you sinners, and purify your hearts, you double-minded.
James 4:8

The hardness of our hearts or "strongholds" causes insensitivity that breaks up relationships. A circle of demons protect the "stronghold—scar tissue." Their plan is to harden your heart so that you only hear what is going on in the realm of darkness. Sadly the person with the scar tissue doesn't even know that they have it. Because they are blind, and they cannot hear. They only hear "self." But praise YHVH, He gave His only Son for us, and all we need to do is to call upon Him.

"My children are in a deep sleep in the lap of the wicked one. I want My Bride to be awake, watchful, diligent, for a time of change is at hand. Holy Spirit will guide you. My hand is always upon you, I will give you renewed strength for what I've planned for you. My peace will fill your mind, and My love will be your daily portion. Remember I am the Lord Your God, and in Me you have no limitations. Don't ponder on all the "whys," give them to Me, because I use everything in your life to transform you into My likeness. I am your guide take My hand. Come like a child, I AM your Abba Father." Yes, life is challenging, but let's overcome by living in His presence.

Reflection:
* Is your scar tissue preventing you from hearing anything but your pain?
* If so it is time to draw near to YHVH and then He will *come near to you.*

Response:
Are you going to stay where you are or take the step back to YHVH?

Dwelling in His shelter

Whoever dwells in the shelter of the Most High will rest in the shadow
of the Almighty. I will say of the Lord,
"He is my refuge and my fortress, my God, in whom I trust."
Psalm 91:1-2

When we walk in the shelter of and the abiding presence of YHVH, we will choose not to live a life of compromise. Time and again I see how the evil that hides in brokenness, the lust of the world and even our selfish love destroys people's lives. You will either destroy your strongholds through the Blood of Yeshua or the strongholds will destroy you. We have to take up our responsibility for the condition of our lives and for those of our children. This means that I cannot continue living in denial.

In the shelter of the Most High you will be confronted with your darkness. Holy Spirit will show you all your denial and you will learn to face the truth about yourself. People always want an easy solution to their problems: But, there isn't one, you have to deal with all the darkness and face the pain. It is done layer by layer. Yes, we need to be patient, just as Yeshua is patient with us. If we can only see the condition of so many of our children's lives, then we as parents will take up our responsibility! This condition cannot be fixed with money. I read the emails I receive and my heart cries out—let us make a choice today to choose Life!

Reflection:
- Are you taking the easy route and throwing money at the problems your children have?
- Your pain and your family's pain will be healed in the shelter of YHVH's presence.

Response:
Choose Life today. Choose to dwell in the shelter of the Most High.

Seated in Heavenly places

*But because of his great love for us, God, who is rich in mercy, made us alive with
Christ even when we were dead in transgressions—it is by grace you have been saved.
And God raised us up with Christ and seated us with him
in the heavenly realms in Christ Jesus.*
Ephesians 2:4-6

We need to take up our seat in Heavenly places. We need to choose to no longer live a divided life, also living in the valley of death and hell. People love to proclaim, *"We are seated us with him in the heavenly realms in Christ Jesus,* but without any proof of this being visible or evident in their lives. I hear how they say, "All hell has been let loose!" What they don't realize is that yes, the seal came off, because the trigger was pulled and whatever was in them or someone else came spilling out.

Our whole spirit needs to function out of the Heavenly place—the shelter of the Most High. This is where we need to be living our lives covered by His divine protection and peace. Holy Spirit never just instructs us into truth, no, He always teaches us, and then "leads" us into truth. Even if it is through the dark storms of life and sometimes even through the darkness in us that stands up against His Light. After Yeshua was baptized by John, His son-ship was affirmed by YHVH. *Then He was "led" into the wilderness. Then Jesus was led by the Spirit into the wilderness to be tempted by the devil* (Matthew 4:1). Yeshua often speaks to us through the leading of Holy Spirit.

Reflection:
* Do you want the gain without the pain? In the Christian life this is not possible.
* Dwelling in Heavenly places in the shelter of the Most High means that you will be led by Holy Spirit.

Response:
Repent before YHVH about your resistance to being "led" by Holy Spirit in all things.

Led by Holy Spirit

Jesus, full of the Holy Spirit, left the Jordan and was led by the Spirit
into the wilderness, where for forty days he was tempted by the devil.
Luke 4:1-2a

When we hear the words, "led by Holy Spirit," we never like to think that we are led by Holy Spirit to face our giants; or we are being "led" by Holy Spirit to remove the darkness out of us. Before Yeshua was "led" into doing miracles, He was "led" by Holy Spirit into battle; and this war was over the purity of His heart. His character was proven through conflict.

The word "tempted" means to be tested or proven. These words are so significantly deep to me. Yeshua was always without sin, yet He learned obedience through the things He suffered! As the Son of YHVH He had to suffer! Yes, and likewise we have to go through difficulties. Abba Father is never afraid that we won't make it. He knows that as long as we call out to Him and stay in the shelter of His abiding presence He will cover us and protect us. He knows that after a certain degree of brokenness we are so much more useable as a vessel of honor. When you come out of your denial, it feels like brokenness. But, it is only the thick walls of denial that are breaking. Only then can Holy Spirit go to the real brokenness and the root of your pain.

Reflection:

- Where do you find yourself in your process of moving towards wholeness?
- Are you beginning to view your testing from the perspective of YHVH's love for you?

Response:

Will you choose YHVH's abiding presence or run back to hide behind the scar tissue of your wounds?

Remain in Yeshua

*"I am the true vine, and my Father is the gardener." "I am the vine; you are the branches.
If you remain in me and I in you, you will bear much fruit; apart from me you can do nothing."*
John 15:1&5

To receive shelter from someone, you need to stand close to that person. Yeshua asks us to choose be one with Him. I am the Vine, He says, and you are the branches— being one with Him grants me divine protection. We need to stand against sin and a life of compromise. We need to choose Truth and Light. If not, we live a double life and every part of us will not be under His divine protection. How many times over the years have we deceived ourselves about the quality of our Christian walk?

Our Christian lives are made up of learning lessons and then passing tests; or possibly writing and rewriting tests as often as are deemed necessary. These tests are never about mere knowledge, but focus on us learning the lesson and appropriating it into our lives. This is a heart that is changed into the likeness of YHVH. It produces a contented heart, a heart filled with love and peace in the midst of the most difficult situations. Don't ever fear the fires of life. Yeshua will always be with us even n our trials. Just keep on calling out to Him. We need to become whole and one with H m. We need to come under the divine protection of the Most High God—El Elyon.

Reflection:

* Are you resistant to the notion of being constantly tested as you learn lessons?
* How close are you to YHVH right now? Only by constantly abiding in Yeshua will you bear fruit.

Response:

You will only triumph in your trials through abiding. Bearing fruit and abiding go hand in hand.

Living Waters will flow

Then we will see how the Living Waters begin flowing out from our innermost beings. People will be able to drink from these waters and not from our doctrines. Our children look at our lives, more than they listen to our words. I can see how all these tests in life "lead" us into maturity. We are all like a well and whatever is in us will come out of us. We can only feed people from what we have inside of us. And that my friend, is what our children taste every day. *"Yeshua, please help me to keep my heart turned towards You. Please strip away my self-deception. Take away my veils of denial, dismiss all my excuses. I humble myself before You, please take control of my life and always lead me by Your Spirit into the shelter of Your love."

I want to encourage you today to run the race of faith, don't stop! It is a race, and Yeshua will help us until the very end. Aldo said to me; "Mom, thank you that you always help and pray for me, please don't stop Mom!" I just smiled. *For his anger lasts only a moment, but his favor lasts a lifetime; weeping may stay for the night, but rejoicing comes in the morning* (Psalm 30:5).

Reflection:

- What is flowing from your life: Life or death; Living Water or stagnant water?
- Are you able to see how the tests in your life are leading you to maturity?

Response:

Pray the prayer in the first paragraph* to Yeshua.

Treasure in jars of clay

But we have this treasure in jars of clay to show that
this all-surpassing power is from God and not from us.
2 Corinthians 4:7

We all have this treasure inside of us—Christ within us, our hope of Glory. The treasure spoken about in second Corinthians is YHVH within us. This means that all the treasures of Heaven are ours as a gift to partake of and to share with others. But they are held in simple earthen vessels; they are held in you and me, in all of our frailty. This is so that we will not become puffed up, knowing that the power is YHVH's. How often do we see this "treasure" in other people? Or do we only look at them in order to find fault and to judge what the eye can see?

I have learned so much from Aldo who is so humble and just himself. He loves YHVH and is totally dependent upon Him. I wonder many times if it is not our puffed up lives that keep us so distant from the King. I consider myself to be so very privileged to walk this journey with Aldo, and to be trained by YHVH through Holy Spirit on this walk of faith. The walk of faith is always a walk in the realm of the supernatural. That is where you will learn to seek the treasures within, and not to ignore and disregard the person because he is not as able as you are!

Reflection:
- How much of the treasure is evident in your life and what are you doing with it?
- When you look at others is it to judge them or to acknowledge YHVH at work in them?

Response:
Thank YHVH for this precious treasure He has entrusted to you and for His great power in your life.

The Glory of His presence

For the earth will be filled with the knowledge of
the glory of the Lord as the waters cover the sea.
Habakkuk 2:14

In the mornings I have the privilege of running up the mountain and then sitting in stillness in the glory and presence of YHVH. This morning I ran up to the top and sat down looking out over the beautiful mountains and trees into the distance. The skies and the heavens were spread out like a canopy over the earth, and I heard my Abba say, "I cover you every day like the heavens cover the earth." The wind is blowing today and I know it is as a result of YHVH's command. Even the seas are held within their banks at His Word. It doesn't matter how the seas roar and spray, all things are held together within their boundaries through His power and majesty. This is how safe we are in Him, even if life sometimes roars around us.

Sitting on a rock I heard His soft gentle voice. "I AM the beginning and the end. Retah, nothing is hidden from Me, all is held in the palm of My hand. All the beauty surrounding you, all you can see, was made as a gift, a habitation in which to dwell and to experience My great love for you." How thankful I am to be in this new season of my life were I can enjoy this beauty.

Reflection:

*   Are you so caught up in the busyness of life that you are missing out on being in YHVH's presence?
*   When last have you stopped and spent time luxuriating in the fact that His Glory fills the earth?

Response:

Write a prayer of praise to YHVH thanking Him that you can rest in His love and presence.

Mountain of strength

Send me your light and your faithful care, let them lead me;
let them bring me to your holy mountain, to the place where you dwell.
Psalm 43:3

Every circumstance we experience becomes but a drop in the ocean when we consider who YHVH is. "I AM a Mountain of strength in your day of need. I see how your problems are your mountains. But, by faith I want you to speak to your mountains. I want you to climb your mountain and overcome your fears. Even your setbacks are a wonderful tool in My hands to teach and instruct you in the way you should go. But, will you let Me? Will you climb the mountain with Me? And the fitter you become; the more you will trust Me—until you will be able to run up the mountain. You will experience My grace, mercy and love. When you get lost and call to Me, I will put you back on the right path. As you see Me acting on your behalf our relationship will grow deeper and deeper. When you experience My grace in your life, it will deepen the knowledge of My love for you in your heart."

Sometime ago I took two friends who were visiting me up the mountain. It was steep and difficult, and one of my dear friends said, "When I could not carry on I just called out to YHVH and it felt like the wind helped me up." And so we reached the top.

Reflection:

- Where do you find your strength in times of trouble?
- Could the reason that you are struggling so much be that you are not running to your Strong Mountain?

Response:

Thank YHVH that He is your Strong Mountain in times of trouble.
Ask Him to help you in your time of need.

Persevere to the end

*You need to persevere so that when you have done
the will of God, you will receive what he has promised.*
Hebrews 10:36

I have learned that YHVH uses everything in our lives. Even the bad things He reshapes and molds to our advantage. When my friends and I reached the top of the mountain it was so beautiful. Even though my friend wondered if she would make it, she did! The process of persevering even though tired and then reaching the top grew her confidence as she discovered that she can do all things through Christ who strengthens her. What a good team we make with Yeshua on our side!

She had a blister on her foot and the downhill awaited. I knew it would be painful, but sometimes you have to learn to focus on the end goal rather than the pain. In my life I have had to walk through many blisters in the spirit. I had to keep on walking knowing that with my eyes fixed on the King I would overcome! Many people make their pain their god and then they do not make it to the top. Life has taught me so much about enduring. But, you have to have a vision, an expectation! You become what you gaze upon. Look up and see the heavens. Look around you and absorb the beauty of the surroundings in your life. They are the declaration of YHVH's love and capability.

Reflection:

*   Can you testify to YHVH reshaping and molding even the bad things to your advantage?
*   If you are in a difficult place then look to Him and choose to persevere.

Response:

Thank YHVH for His love and faithfulness to you. He will never forsake you—so trust in Him.

Walk in His presence

Blessed are those who have learned to acclaim you,
who walk in the light of your presence, LORD.
Psalm 89:15

In the mornings I take Aldo for a walk on our street. Spontaneously he worships, bringing a song of love to His King. It is not easy for me because he is so much bigger and stronger than I am, but what a joy it is to walk with him. On our way we pass a house where students live. Every day we see the same young people coming out of their house on their way to university. I no longer feel sorry for myself, I now rejoice in our situation.

Today, a young man, who always sees us walking, came up to Aldo and greeted him. "Morning, what is your name?" and he introduced himself. We had a little chat and off we went. Aldo said, "Mom, did you see the Light in him? That is why he greeted me, it was the King who told him to greet me." It made Aldo's day. He smiled knowing that he is special to his Abba. We got home and he went down to their flat and started to pray and work on the computer. I went to see how he was doing; "I also study, just like them mom." Even if his life is limited in so many ways, he just loves every moment and he still looks up and sees the beauty.

Reflection:
- If you are going through difficulties you can know that you are not alone.
- The question is what do you focus on your difficulties or on your King?

Response:
Instead of complaining today choose to praise Abba Father, who is your King, for His love and goodness.

The Court of Heaven

Therefore let us [with privilege] approach the throne of grace [that is, the throne of God's gracious favor] with confidence and without fear, so that we may receive mercy [for our failures] and find [His amazing] grace to help in time of need [an appropriate blessing, coming just at the right moment].
Hebrews 4:16 [AMPLIFIED BIBLE]

When we pray we open the door to the Throne room. Prayer is like a key for us. *Let us then approach God's throne of grace with confidence, so that we may receive mercy and find grace to help us in our time of need.* Yeshua paid the full price for us to enter in. The veil has been torn apart. But the choice is still ours whether we are going in with prayer or not. We can go as deep as the Court in Heaven where you can bring your petition before YHVH.

Prayers like petitions and intercession do not happen on the battlefield, but in the Court Room. It is a process that occurs and proceeds before the Court of Heaven and is a legal transaction before the Judge of the entire universe. If you are serious about your case then you will go to the Court in Heaven and bring it before the Judge. In the Court there is a different protocol than on the battlefield. It is most important to gather all your legal facts (in the Light), so that you will have a breakthrough and not a backlash. Maybe it is our lack of understanding and what is really hiding in us that makes us so easily plead "not guilty" in this Court.

Reflection:
*   Where do you go when you are in need: to human resources or to the Court in Heaven?
*   Do you take approaching the Throne of Grace seriously?

Response:
Thank Yeshua that His death on the Cross has bought you access to the Throne of Grace.

____

____

____

____

____

____

____

____

Blessing or curse?

This day I call the heavens and the earth as witnesses against you that I have set before you life and death, blessings and curses. Now choose life, so that you and your children may live.

Deuteronomy 30:19

Satan is accusing and declaring curses upon people and he is also waiting for a witness. Our words and our deeds give him the power to put curses upon people. So who will prevail? The one with whom we will agree. I have to make choices every day. Yeshua holds before me life or death, blessing or cursing—I have to choose. What are the documents in my hands when I enter the court? Do I cooperate with the great Intercessor and become an intercessor? Do I forgive 70 x 7 times, or will I side with Satan and become an accuser of the brethren?

I forgive and ask forgiveness for my secret angry thoughts and my own sin, only then can I put my case in YHVH's hands. *Therefore, since we have a great high priest who has ascended into heaven, Jesus the Son of God... Let us then approach God's throne of grace with confidence* (Hebrews 4:14a&16a). Remember there is a difference between prayer and petition *and pray in the Spirit on all occasions with all kinds of prayers and requests* (Ephesians 6:18a). Prayer covers all aspects of requests. And a petition is defined as a formal written request that is presented to a superior authority. It is a legal presentation before the Judge, requesting judicial action, a verdict from Heaven's Court.

Reflection:
* Are you being used to bring blessings or curses into peoples' lives?
* If the latter could this be the reason that your petitions are not being granted?

Response:
Choose Life today, choose to be a blessing! Choose to obey YHVH so that your children may live.

Where is your hope?

Guide me in your truth and teach me, for you are God
my Savior, and my hope is in you all day long.
Psalm 25:5

We all expect many things in and from life, but our expectations don't always turn out the way we hoped and planned. If our expectations are based on events, circumstances or things, we are headed for great disappointment. What about when what I face is not so favorable? If we really want to see YHVH's work in our lives, we have to raise our level of expectation to having complete faith in YHVH and not being dependent on our own abilities and ways.

Life is so much more than just getting what you want. It is more than getting up and going to work every day, having the best car or home, or even going on a great vacation. Life is so much more than our constant focus on accumulating more and more stuff, on having all that our eyes see and desire! Have you found real life yet? The God–kind of expectation goes far beyond events, or the perfect circumstances. It is not rooted in things that I have control over. It is rooted in a supernatural force that only comes from having faith in YHVH and His Word. It is from the inside out. It comes when you are anchored in Him, having complete faith in Him and His abilities. It comes from resting in Him and abiding in His presence.

Reflection:
- Are you frantically running around placing your hope in material things?
- YHVH offers you rest from your striving. Come to Him and place your hope in Him today.

Response:
Kneel in YHVH's presence allowing Holy Spirit to minister to you.

Faith and Righteousness

What does Scripture say? "Abraham believed God,
and it was credited to him as righteousness."
Romans 4:3

Because the God-kind of expectation is not based on natural things, you can never become discouraged. You keep on expecting the best that Yeshua has in store for you, while you do your best. In this you come to understand that delays and disappointments are not there to discourage you, because your eyes are on Yeshua and not on the situation or circumstances. You are rooted and grounded in Christ and you are anchored in His love and joy.

You will keep on trusting and expecting the best that Yeshua has in store for you, even when the situation looks impossible because He is the God who rules over the impossible. He is El Shadai, the God who is Almighty! Abraham had this kind of expectation. (Romans 4:18). We refer to this as "The God-kind of expectation." Whether you see, or don't see, you keep on trusting that YHVH will make a way! Maybe not the way you planned, but His plans for us are always the best! In the natural realm, Abraham didn't have any reason to hope. His situation truly looked impossible. But his expectations were not based in the natural realm, they were based on YHVH's promises. And that is why he kept his hope and his faith in YHVH. He kept his hope regardless of what he saw.

Reflection:

- There is blessing in believing and trusting YHVH—in having a God-kind of expectation.
- What He has for us is so much better than our ideas and dreams.

Response:

Lay your plans down at the foot of the Cross and commit yourself to YHVH's plans for your life.

His ways are better

"For My thoughts are not your thoughts,
nor are your ways My ways," says the Lord.
Isaiah 55:8 [NEW KING JAMES VERSION]

Every day we face situations. But, I have learned to live my life in another realm—the realm of the supernatural. To live there you need to be anchored in Christ. In this realm you are anchored in "hope, faith and love." "Hope" means that you are anchored in and understand the fact that YHVH is true to His Word. It means that you are holding on to the YHVH who has the power to overrule everything. Doing things His way! This is the God–kind of expectation. This is such an incredible walk—because I always see and taste far more than I had hoped for. YHVH is no man that He could lie.

When we have our expectations anchored in Yeshua we will not be moved by how we feel, or what things look like. You have to move into another realm, the realm of faith in Yeshua our King. His ways are far better than our ways. All He asks of us is to surrender everything into His hands, trusting Him and using our words to create life and not death, obeying His voice and living life to the full. Life is not about us, it is all about Him! *Let us hold fast the confession of our hope without wavering, for He who promised is faithful* (Hebrews 10:23 NKJV).

Reflection:
- Are you frustrated because you are living your life your way and not in YHVH's presence?
- Take a truthful look at where you find yourself in your walk with Him.

Response:
What are you going to do about what Holy Spirit has shown you today?

Heart, soul and mind

*Love the Lord your God with all your heart
and with all your soul and with all your strength.*
Deuteronomy 6:5

In Matthew 22:37-38 Jesus replied: *"'Love the Lord your God with all your heart and with all your soul and with all your mind.' This is the first and greatest commandment."* (LOVE GOD). To have us love Him is YHVH's highest priority, forever. YHVH is Love, wholehearted Love. (1 John 4:16). This is what He wants us to know and to experience— His perfect Love! Yeshua also said: *"As the Father has loved me, so have I loved you. Now remain in my love"* (John 15:9). Just to think that YHVH loves us with the same intensity that He loves Yeshua makes me sit in quiet wonder. YHVH is wholehearted Love! I can ponder on that for days!

How can I love others if I cannot even love YHVH? How can I love others if I cannot even love myself? How can I love if I don't abide in His love? Maybe that is why it is so difficult for us to love someone unconditionally, and wholeheartedly? The world has conditioned us to be perfect and only then will we be loved perfectly. When we have an orphan spirit all our energy goes into being perfect—something that is quite impossible. With this spirit we will never feel loved unless we achieve perfection, and seeing as we never will, we never feel loved.

Reflection:
* Have your eyes been opened as to why you find it so hard to love unconditionally and wholeheartedly?
* Until you love YHVH wholeheartedly and accept His love for you, you won't love others.

Response:
Tell YHVH how much you love Him today, and thank Him that He loves you unconditionally and wholeheartedly.

Trust and submit

*Trust in the Lord with all your heart and lean not on your own understanding;
in all your ways submit to him, and he will make your paths straight.*
Proverbs 3:5-6

Many years ago, after our accident Tinus and I tried everything to help Aldo become the child he was before the accident. We wanted him to be 'perfect' as before. But, he could not, because after a brain injury many things change. We had to do most things for him, and even communication was challenging. Sometimes he couldn't even hold an intelligible conversation. One night, after about five years of battling to get Aldo to be as he was before the accident we spoke to each other and realized that we were not going to get the "old" Aldo back. I told Tinus that we needed to repent to Yeshua, and we needed to accept Aldo as he is today. We need to bury our "old child," and embrace the "new Aldo."

We prayed, and asked for forgiveness. I could hear my Abba's soft gentle voice, "Retah, I love you wholeheartedly. And if you abide in My love, you will never expect anyone to be perfect before you can love them unconditionally. You will love the way I love if you abide in My love! Just abide in My love My child, and your life will never be the same. You will look through My eyes, touch with My hands, bless the way I bless, and love the way I love."

Reflection:
*   Do you have a situation in your life that you are battling to accept?
*   I hope you will be encouraged by our experience and that YHVH will use it to help you.

Response:
Bring your battle to YHVH and ask Him to shine His Light of Love on it.
Then surrender it to Him.

Perfect Love

*There is no fear in love. But perfect love drives out fear, because fear
has to do with punishment. The one who fears is not made perfect in love.*
1 John 4:18

Very early the next morning Aldo came to our room. He struggled to walk on his own, so we could hear him approaching, falling over things in the passage. He fell onto our bed, and looked at us. He said, "I am crying now." (He cannot cry, he has no tears so he always tells us when he cries.) "Why are you crying Aldo?" "I saw you and Dad last night before the Throne, where you asked Abba Father to forgive you and to help you to accept me just the way I am. Thank you that you will love me now, even if I am not perfect." We all cried and held each other. (Your children sense if you don't love them unconditionally. Most parents' love come with conditions attached.)

That was the beginning of a new chapter in our lives. Abide in the Father's love, and you will be able to love perfectly. I know today that it is impossible if you do not abide in the Fathers love! If you look through your fleshly eyes you will always be able to find fault in people. Today Tinus will walk with Aldo, his arm around his shoulders to support him. I see how he often looks him in the eyes and says, "Aldo you are my son, and I am so proud to be your father!"

Reflection:

* What has YHVH said to you through this experience that we went through?
* Are you open to loving the people in your life unconditionally or are you struggling with this?

Response:

Take some time to write about the emotions that have surfaced through this.

Yeshua's love for us

And walk in the way of love, just as Christ loved us and gave himself up for us as a fragrant offering and sacrifice to God.
Ephesians 5:2

There is no greater thing that we can ask for than the love of YHVH in Yeshua. Everything in life flows from this love. If you seek wisdom, knowledge, acceptance, and to be acknowledged you have only gained a portion. I look at Solomon and see how his wisdom went astray, and his knowledge led to pride! But the love of Yeshua surpasses all this. What brings meaning to your life? Your life partner, your children, wealth, relationships, sports, or spiritual experiences? We all have a deep longing inside of us. Unless you fill the longing with the love of Yeshua it will be filled with other things that will not fulfil you, and you will be led astray.

The enemy climbs into the deep secret pain (longings) of the heart. When you feel that you do not belong he starts to fill you with evil fleshly desires, fleshly dreams and thoughts. Out of this place he starts to rule your life. The evil thoughts become memories that play over and over in your mind. Memories carry emotions, and the emotions become actions. It is all born out of pain, disappointments and anger. Anger about what people did to you. You trusted man so much, you needed acceptance so badly, and now you find yourself playing the blaming game alone. Run to your safe place in YHVH's presence.

Reflection:
* Have you been deeply disappointed and angered by the things people have done to you?
* What are you doing with that anger in the light of Yeshua's love for you?

Response:
Other things and people will always fail you, but Yeshua never will.
Thank Him for this today.

Run the race

Therefore, since we are surrounded by such a great cloud of witnesses, let us throw off everything that hinders and the sin that so easily entangles. And let us run with perseverance the race marked out for us.
Hebrews 12:1

If you carry hidden hate then hidden curses will come out of your heart, and you will become a bitter person. How can man be so dependent on people's acceptance? Forgive those who hurt you, you don't need to walk the same path as them. But we need to forgive! We must be rooted and grounded in Yeshua's love and acceptance. We must have this foundation in our lives. To be grounded in YHVH's love comes from Salvation. Christ dwelling by faith in our hearts.

Then I won't measure myself against others, I will not try to find favor with man, but I will be secure in knowing that I am a child of God. He loves me, and He is proud to call me "son or daughter." *Blessed are those whose strength is in you* (Psalm 84:5a). These are the life lessons that I teach my family and myself. Always be anchored in the love and acceptance of YHVH, not in man's acceptance. Remember your strength is in Him, not in yourself or who you know! Trade your pain and sorrow daily—receiving instead Yeshua's healing and joy. Set your heart steadfastly on the call that Yeshua has placed on your life. Run the race of faith, run and don't murmur. Be joyful and thankful, you have so much to be grateful for.

Reflection:
* Are you running your race in YHVH's presence seeking only to please Him?
* If not then it is time that you took a serious look inside your heart.

Response:
Ask Holy Spirit to shine the Light of His presence into your heart to illuminate the dark places.

Pray and believe

"Therefore I tell you, whatever you ask for in prayer,
believe that you have received it, and it will be yours."
Mark 11:24

have learned to constantly affirm my faith in YHVH, even in the face of the storms. YHVH has heard my prayer. I know because His Word assures me of this. And this is when results come: You see the result, you declare the result, you believe the result, and you receive the result. The "believing" always comes before the receiving. Think carefully before you speak. If you know YHVH, you will know that you are never alone; you don't need to be afraid. *"Never will I leave you; never will I forsake you."* So we say with confidence, *"The Lord is my helper"* (Hebrews 13:5c-6a).

Let's start speaking words of faith. Keep on believing and see it come to pass. See the results, and receive the results. Don't look to man for help, focus on YHVH—He is your Help! Keep your thinking in line with His will, and your "beliefs" will be according to His will. Speak life over people and bless and pray for them: Because what you do, speak and think about others will be done to you. That is what His Word says. Faith declares the answer, and believes the answer, then sees the answer. Real faith in YHVH simply says about you what the Word of God says about you. We have what the Word says we have.

Reflection:
- What has YHVH been saying to you about living in His presence? Have you obeyed?
- Take hold by faith of what you are trusting YHVH for today.

Response:
Say it and believe it: Yeshua is my Helper, my Healer, my Deliverer, and my Provider.

*Now faith is confidence in what we hope for
and assurance about what we do not see.
This is what the ancients were commended for.
By faith we understand that the universe was formed
at God's command, so that what is seen
was not made out of what was visible.*
Hebrews 11:1-3

Walking by Faith

For in the gospel
the righteousness of God is revealed—
a righteousness that is by faith from first to last,
just as it is written:
"The righteous will live by faith."
Romans 1:17

A walk of faith

But he gives us more grace. That is why Scripture says:
"God opposes the proud but shows favor to the humble."
James 4:6

A walk of faith is filled with trials, tests and battles. But as a result we learn more about Yeshua and about life. In my faith-walk I am determined to become progressively more sensitive to Yeshua's will. My goal is to follow His guidance each and every day. In other words my prayers for healing in our lives (body, soul and spirit) become a fresh dedication of my life to Yeshua and His Kingdom every day.

I have learnt to allow YHVH to do whatever He wills with my life. Each year He trusts me with more. Of myself I would never have dared to do many of the things He has led me to do. I would never have attempted them in my own strength and human wisdom. I can declare today that being on a spiritual adventure with the Lord Jesus Christ, Yeshua our Messiah, is the most humbling, beautiful, and life changing experience anyone can ever know. It is the only way to live a life of perfect peace in the midst of all the storms that life brings our way. YHVH is the way and He opens each door that He wants you to walk through. The key is to walk by faith and to understand that on our own we can do nothing.

Reflection:
- Where are you in your walk of faith? Is something holding you back from stepping out?
- Think about where you are right now. What do you need to do to humble yourself so that YHVH can have His way in your life.

Response:
Write a prayer to YHVH telling Him where you are, what is holding you back, and what you desire.

Living by faith

For we live by faith, not by sight.
2 Corinthians 5:7

When Tinus and I climbed Mount Kilimanjaro I realized that it is a picture of our lives. Every day brings new, unknown territory and every day comes with new challenges. As we grow in Christ we are being exposed to deeper dimensions in the spirit which is always challenging because of its unfamiliarity. What most people don't realize is that everything that happens in the physical has a spiritual root. So your journey is actually a spiritual journey.

With every step of faith we take we grow and progress in the spirit. And the more we die to self and our own desires and agendas the stronger we become in the spirit. Yes, that is how YHVH's Kingdom works. It is totally opposite to the world's agenda and standards. In the spirit we only progress when we die to self, love unconditionally and when we serve others without expecting something in return. "Self" is a hindrance in our spiritual climb. As Tinus struggled to breathe on the mountain, he cried out to Abba, "please help me." And, He gave him breath for two steps, after which Tinus stopped and had to ask for help again. That night Tinus said, "Retah, I once again realized that I cannot even breathe without YHVH. He wants us to be totally dependent on Him alone."

Reflection:
*   Are you climbing a steep mountain in your life right now?
*   Are you trying to do it in your own strength or in Yeshua's?

Response:
Realize that you cannot conquer your mountain on your own.
Walk by faith and not by sight.

The power of words

These things we also speak, not in words which man's wisdom teaches but which the Holy Spirit teaches, comparing spiritual things with spiritual.
1 Corinthians 2:13 [NEW KING JAMES VERSION]

I have learned in my life that the one thing that is worse than prayerlessness, is praying without expectation. We all want answers, but the answer lies in the prayer. There are not many people willing to take the time or make the effort to go on their knees, constantly seeking YHVH's face until there is a breakthrough in the situation they are praying about.

I read how the Disciples looked at the boy with the demon and they had no answers. Yeshua looked at the same boy and His concern was not the demon or the boy, but the unbelief of His Disciples. He could see how the spirits of unbelief worked through them. The Disciples' questions were about casting out the demon, but Yeshua knew that when unbelief was cast out, the rest would follow. Faith is the key to powerful prayer. The enemy uses our unbelief against us. He can also use other people's unbelief against us. Learning this has forced me into a place where I started to protect my family and my life by not sharing everything that I am trusting God for. Carelessness about who we speak to can harm us. We do not realize that people's unbelief affects us and is used by the enemy. Their words of unbelief are very powerful in the spirit.

Reflection:
- If you have difficulty with a breakthrough is it because you lack expectation?
- Have you been used by the enemy against someone as a result of negative words you have spoken?

Response:
Change the way you pray and begin to pray with the Spirit's wisdom.

Guard your words

So then faith comes by hearing, and hearing by the word of God.
Romans 10:17 [NEW KING JAMES VERSION]

I have often seen in our journey with Aldo and Chantelle how people's unbelief has exposed the true condition of their hearts through their critical comments. YHVH was still faithful in His promises, but today I know how people's words of unbelief are used by the enemy to fight against us. Even Peter did an interesting thing in Acts 9: *But Peter put them all out, and knelt down and prayed. And turning to the body he said, "Tabitha, arise." And she opened her eyes, and when she saw Peter she sat up. Then he gave her his hand and lifted her up; and when he had called the saints and widows, he presented her alive* (Vs40-41 NKJV). Do you think that Peter could have been countering the unbelief of the people around him; and he wanted nothing to stand in the way of his prayer to YHVH?

We have to pray with bold confidence and expectancy. When YHVH hears this kind of prayer, He always reveals His power and Wisdom to His children in the most phenomenal ways. I am just a normal mom, fighting the same things that many other mothers and fathers face. I know how much I love YHVH, but still I have to fight to get completely free from the giants that would stop me entering into the Promised Land.

Reflection:
- Don't let other people steal your blessing through their negative words.
- Faith comes by hearing, so speak out in faith, trusting in YHVH's Word.

Response:
Choose to focus on the positive and speak out in faith as you pray to YHVH now.

Hear my prayer

Hear me when I call, O God of my righteousness! You have relieved me in my distress; Have mercy on me, and hear my prayer.
Psalm 4:1 [NEW KING JAMES VERSION]

I walk a journey with Chantelle, as she fights generational depression. It is literally a fight and I see it coming. Then we pray, and pray, but after many times around the same mountain, I really cried out to YHVH, "What more Lord?!" I waited expectantly to hear from Him. People don't want to hear "pray this prayer, or break this curse, keep on praying, keep on seeking." Instead they want a quick fix.

I did not say anything to anyone; I just prayed and sought YHVH for help. She is my daughter now, and I will fight for her! I will not accept this as normal. Not in my house! As I was running on the mountain one day, speaking and crying out to Him, YHVH spoke to me; "Lewis curse." I had no idea where I had heard this before. When I got home Aldo wrote, "So Mom, you expected an answer, and now you have heard from Wisdom. Many times I wrote to you that there is a banner of "Harm" over people, and a "vow" in the spirit, but you did not do anything about it? Congratulations Sarah, the Lewis curse is the "harm curse" (freemason, occult) that pays out to people who turn their back on the occult. We have to break the harm curse and the vows Mom."

Reflection:
- Are you or someone close to you battling depression?
- Are you willing to go the distance in trusting and obeying YHVH as He speaks to you?

Response:
Tell YHVH that you want His solution and answer, not man's wisdom or quick fixes.

He is faithful

"Therefore know that the Lord your God, He is God, the faithful God who keeps covenant and mercy for a thousand generations with those who love Him and keep His commandments."

Deuteronomy 7:9 [NEW KING JAMES VERSION]

I knew that YHVH is faithful and that He had heard my prayers and the cry of my heart. He was leading me to the answer that would bring help and healing for Chantelle. After the conversation with Aldo I read from his book that night some of the things that he had previously written. I now had a new, deeper, clearer understanding of what he had written about. "Baal lives in people's minds." "The curse is to cry" (to hurt or harm people in different ways). I then did some research on the internet about the Lewis curse and I found the following: Poverty, infertility, barrenness, and female problems. Breakdowns in relationships. Chronic sickness (heart, bronchial, digestive, circulatory, reproductive etc.) Confusion, mental illness, and insanity. Stuttering, and learning difficulties. Accident proneness, defeat and failure. Emotional hardness, doubt, unbelief, and cynicism. Religious, and controlling spirits. Spiritual blindness to reading or receiving the Word. Woman hating. Stubbornness, pride and arrogance.

It mentioned that Masonic or cult involvement by a person or previous generations in the family line e.g. parents, grandparents etc. can bring upon the successive children an unwanted spiritual inheritance for which they can be held accountable, even to the third and fourth generations. *...visiting the iniquity of the fathers upon the children to the third and fourth generations...* (Deuteronomy 5:9 NKJV).

Reflection:

- It doesn't matter what we face we don't have to fear because YHVH is with us.
- He promises us that He will keep His covenant with us for a thousand generations.

Response:

YHVH wants you and your family to be clean vessels available to be used by Him.

A Light is shining

The people who walked in darkness have seen a great light; those who dwelt in the land of the shadow of death, upon them a light has shined.
Isaiah 9:2 [NEW KING JAMES VERSION]

My first thoughts were that we had prayed the Freemason repentance prayer many years ago? Then I realized that at the time we did not cleanse our seed, our spiritual DNA before we prayed the prayer. And the "Lewis curse" needs to be broken separately from the Freemason prayer. The aim of the curse is to hurt those who turn their backs on the cult or Freemasonry. I had nothing to lose, so I immediately started to pray in a childlike manner; "Father, I come and I break the curse and the vows..." as Holy Spirit showed me I just kept on praying by faith as YHVH led me.

That night I read what Aldo had written during that day and what an amazing surprise I found. "Mom, you have prayed and the dart (curse) was cancelled." "Chans' walls (mind) are Light; she is saved from the curse of "becoming a wound." "I am amazed, Chans is Light!" "Wisdom says her agony is out." "Wow, her "cry" curse is out! You really love Chans Mom." "Well done, you've learned a lot Mom" "Asthma is out of Josh now" (Wow, I didn't realize that Aldo even knew that Josh had suffered from asthma). "Darkness is out, crying is out." "Our dark inheritance (spiritual inheritance) is out, I am so thankful."

Reflection:
* As you walk in faith you can know that YHVH will always lead you into the Light.
* You do not need to fear the enemy he cannot keep a hold on you or your loved ones.

Response:
Ask YHVH to help you with any situations that you have in your life that are robbing you of blessing.

Enter the Promised Land

Do what is right and good in the Lord's sight, so that it may go well with you and you may go in and take over the good land the Lord promised on oath to your ancestors.
Deuteronomy 6:18

After this experience I knew for sure that we can never stop fighting and praying. And yes, there are many, many people who confront me, and ask, "Why do I have to keep on praying and repenting?" I look at all of our lives, and our children's lives, and I wonder how it is that they cannot see the fruits of destruction that are all around us? What do you have to lose? I broke this curse that was over us and all the broken parts of our heart (broken wounds) and immediately afterwards Aldo wrote to me, "The curse is broken!"

For the first time Chantelle and I can visit her wounds together. There s Light inside of her, and she is willing to speak and allow Holy Spirit into her wounds. Before the prayer she could not do this. That does not mean that we do not have to deal with our pain anymore, but it helps a great deal if the stronghold or curses are broken and the wounds opened in order to receive healing from Yeshua. All the glory to YHVH, Yeshua's Blood and Wisdom for teaching us and never giving up on us! This is our journey, and I will not stop fighting to possess the FULLNESS of the Promised Land that YHVH has promised us if we walk by faith.

Reflection:

- YHVH instructs us to do what is right and good in His sight.
- If we do this He promises that everything will go well with us and we will enter the Promised Land.

Response:

Declare aloud your intention to walk by Faith in YHVH's ways today so that it may go well with you.

YHVH has a plan

"For I know the plans I have for you," declares the Lord, "plans to prosper you and not to harm you, plans to give you hope and a future."
Jeremiah 29:11

Many people come from a "present day Egypt" with all its sin and idolatry. If you are born into a cult it is not easy to leave "Egypt" and possess the Promised Land that we now have in Yeshua with YHVH. We have the Cross and Yeshua's Resurrection today. But, it remains a battle to partake of and inhabit the Promised Land. Our problem is that we do not understand the bondage of being born into a cult family. We survived, but we are unable to reach the full potential that YHVH desires for us, worshiping YHVH in spirit and truth as our Creator.

Today, I want to assure you, YHVH hears the cry of your heart—He hears a mother and father's prayers. Many people do not even know the extent of their bondage. People who cannot worship YHVH are people who cannot serve Him either. Each time Moses went before Pharaoh he repeated YHVH's request, "Let My people go so that they may serve Me." This serving is worship. YHVH has more for you than aimlessly wandering around the wilderness. He has a purpose and a plan. People become weary, and think there is no escape, but this is a lie! Many choose to stay in the Wilderness; or to keep on going back, no! YHVH has an amazing plan for your life!

Reflection:
- If you feel as if you are wandering around and around in the wilderness don't despair.
- YHVH has a plan for your life and He will deliver you so that you can walk in faith with Him.

Response:
Pour your heart out to YHVH. Tell Him that you want to serve and worship only Him.

Reap what you sow

Do not be deceived, God is not mocked;
for whatever a man sows, that he will also reap.
Galatians 6:7 [NEW KING JAMES VERSION]

Our Abba has planned a perfect life for each one of us. I hear people's cry; "But why is my life in such a mess then? What is His plan?" He knows the plans He has for us. *For I know the thoughts that I think toward you, says the Lord, thoughts of peace and not of evil, to give you a future and a hope* (Jeremiah 29:11 NKJV). We will never be able to find this plan by ourselves. It will always take His help, wisdom and guidance to make the right decisions in our lives. When we surrender and allow Holy Spirit into our choices and pain, then He will add His wisdom to our knowledge and reveal to us greater things than we have ever dreamt of.

In the walk of faith we "grow" into maturity. On this pathway of faith there are many road signs that are named discipline, trust, obedience, unconditional love, dying to self, acknowledging your double life, dealing with your pain, helping those in pain and many more. On this road we sow as we go along, and we always reap in our own lives what we have sown. If we want blessed lives we have to plant the right seeds so that we can harvest blessings.

Reflection:

- If we walk by faith being true to YHVH we will reap a good harvest.
- What sort of a walk have you been on? Is it time to become serious about obeying YHVH?

Response:

YHVH is waiting with all the blessings of Heaven for you to choose to walk by faith with Him.

Sowing and reaping

For he who sows to his flesh will of the flesh reap corruption,
but he who sows to the Spirit will of the Spirit reap everlasting life.
Galatians 6:8 [NEW KING JAMES VERSION]

We reap what we sow in life. I have found that only weeds and wild tares grow without effort. In the darkness of our lives the tares grow wild and are unstoppable. How many of us have sown the wrong seeds in the springtime of our lives, not realizing that unless good seeds and good choices are made we cannot possibly expect good results. Evil seeds can be dark thoughts, evil deeds, a life filled with lies, a double secret life and even painful memories of past hurts.

People's lives are falling apart. Brokenness surfaces more than ever with all the evil seeds becoming evident in our marriages and our children. The fruit is really unpleasant and very bitter for the whole family to eat. The good news is that it is never too late to plough our fields and to root out the weeds. Our Abba wants our lives to be prepared for what He has planned. We have to invite Him into our wounds, even if it is into our darkest weeds. The thoughts we think, the lessons we have learned, the words we speak, the deeds we do, and everything we look at, are all building blocks that we build into our lives. Think about it—every thought and deed, good or bad, comes back to all of us—multiplied.

Reflection:
- If you have sown bad seeds don't try and cover them up—come to YHVH and repent.
- You need to do this not only for your own sake but also for the sake of your family.

Response:
YHVH is a God of mercy and grace, He will never turn us away when we come to Him in repentance.

Glory Light brings healing

Then your light will break forth like the dawn, and your healing will quickly appear; then your righteousness will go before you, and the glory of the Lord will be your rear guard.
Isaiah 58:8

What we are eating today was sown into our lives previously through iniquity, trauma, fear, hate, or by the wrong choices we have made. All of these are the seeds that have been sown in some way into our lives. This is how we as parents sow into our children's lives in the spirit. I see in my own life how my previous double life broke my children and those deeds became the spear in their wounds. Therefore I cannot point a finger at them if I see dark weeds. No, I am the first to take responsibility and say to them, "Please forgive me, I am the reason for this wound in your life. Now I see you do exactly what I did. You hide in a double life. And I am not going to allow Satan to steal your life like he stole mine. Give me your hand, come into the Light (into now-consciousness) and take responsibility for what is manifesting in your life. Let's invite Holy Spirit in."

We confess and repent of all the dark weeds. Then we ask Yeshua to wash us clean with His blood and to heal our wounds. What a joy to see how the Glory Light of YHVH brings healing when the dark seals are opened over our wounds.

Reflection:
* Your children will learn from you. If you take responsibility then so will they.
* Teach them to run towards YHVH's Glory Light, not away from it.

Response:
Bring all your pain and failure to Him and trust Him, in faith, to heal you and your loved ones.

The Light brings healing

But for you who revere my name, the sun of righteousness will rise with healing in its rays. And you will go out and frolic like well-fed calves.
Malachi 4:2

All the ugliness comes out when the seal is lifted off of our wounds. It is only when the seal is removed that we can begin to deal with the hidden demonic spirits inside of us. Not many people are willing to go there. After this you can ask Abba to send His Holy Angels to come and remove all the dead human spirits, familiar spirits and ancient spirits that want to take over your life. These spirits normally hide in the wounds of (all) broken people.

YHVH offers everything we need to build this life in the Light, but He will not force you to accept it. He will wait for you to come to Him, the Architect, to receive His perfect plan. He will guide us with His Word and Holy Spirit, but we still have to do the work. This is where people miss YHVH's plan. They think that because Yeshua did it all they can sit back and look for results. More than ever we have to start to see our brokenness and deal with it. Many adults today have not dealt with their childhood pain and as a result the whole family eats the fruit. This is why I am eager to help my children so that they can walk by faith in the fullness of what Yeshua has planned for them.

Reflection:
- YHVH has given you everything to build your life in the Light—are you utilizing it?
- Walking by Faith means that you hold nothing back from YHVH.

Response:
You are the one who can ensure that your children walk by faith in the plan that YHVH has for them.

Work the plan

Being confident of this, that he who began a good work in you
will carry it on to completion until the day of Christ Jesus.
Philippians 1:6

We had a wonderful architect build our house in Stellenbosch. He drew up the plans, and then we started building otherwise there wouldn t be a house today. I quickly learnt to follow his plans because he knew best. Each day after the builders finished work there was cleaning to do. I am so thankful for everything, now more than ever! I found that it is the things you work for in life that mean the most to you. It is not a quick fix or an overnight success story. It is the same with building your life in Yeshua using His Master-plan. It is a journey, but we have to build and clean up till the end.

To be born again costs you nothing, because Yeshua died for you. But to build your life according to His perfect plan is going to cost you everything! But praise His Holy Name; He gave us Holy Spirit and His Blood. He teaches, He loves, He speaks, He encourages and He will finish the work that He started in us. How I thank Yeshua today that He saved me from my double life. Now, I can have mercy on people who still walk in their dark double life, covered with tears and tares. (Experience has taught me that where there are hidden tears, there are also hidden tares).

Reflection:

* Do you still believe that you, instead of YHVH, know what is best for you and your family?
* Have your battles given you a heart of compassion for other people who are also struggling?

Response:

Thank Yeshua that He has promised to complete the good work He started in you.

Dying to self

I have been crucified with Christ and I no longer live, but Christ lives in me. The life I now live in the body, I live by faith in the Son of God, who loved me and gave himself for me.
Galatians 2:20

The beauty of this journey of faith is that YHVH gives us the grace to die to self because we cannot die by ourselves. I find that this place is the best place I have ever been in. A place of total surrender. Serving the flesh (self) and the sin nature is totally unprofitable. It is only as YHVH opens your spiritual eyes that you will begin to see this new life that He has for you. This is the real life that He desires for us to live in the Spirit. Here we see the glorious works of the Spirit in contrast with all our fleshly works. This is where He takes control of your life, and He provides for all your needs as you humble yourself before Him.

The obedience of a Believer is always motivated by "love." I look at peoples' lives and I see that everyone who is used by YHVH has gone through an experience of dying to self. I have been crucified with Christ and I no longer live, but Christ lives in me. It is not until we know the reality of "death to self" that we can live for Christ, allowing YHVH to truly use us, and to truly bless us. It is all about yielding our will to the will of YHVH.

Reflection:
* Have you come to the place where you are ready to willingly die to self?
* The obedience of a Believer is always motivated by "love." Love for Yeshua.

Response:
If you want to be used by Yeshua then you need to surrender in faith to Him and His will.

The accuser defeated

Then I heard a loud voice in heaven say: "Now have come the salvation and the power and the kingdom of our God, and the authority of his Messiah. For the accuser of our brothers and sisters, who accuses them before our God day and night, has been hurled down."
Revelation 12:10

We have to make sure that we have repented of what Holy Spirit shows us, before we go to the Court: Because the accuser of the brethren is the one who accuses us day and night, and night and day. So if I am in denial about the true condition of my heart, this Court room event will result in a backlash. There are often secrets in the wounds, so it is best to present my whole being to YHVH and ask Him to search all the secrets so that I can take responsibility for them.

Search me, God, and know my heart; test me and know my anxious thoughts. See if there is any offensive way in me, and lead me in the way everlasting (Psalm 139:23-24). David asked that any secret or unknown sin be exposed so that he could repent and not be found guilty in court. There was a time in my life when the spiritual battles were so intense that I went daily to the Court in Heaven. One day I asked Abba, "Do You mind that I come every day? I am so sorry but I have only You who can help me." He answered me with the Scripture from Psalm 139, and ever since I know the power of presenting my case before the King.

Reflection:

- The good news is that you don't have to walk the faith walk alone.
- You can come as often as you need to before YHVH's throne of grace.

Response:

Pray Psalm 139:23-24 as you bow in YHVH's presence right now.

Yeshua our Intercessor

For we do not have a high priest who is unable to empathize with our weaknesses, but we have one who has been tempted in every way, just as we are—yet he did not sin. Let us then approach God's throne of grace with confidence, so that we may receive mercy and find grace to help us in our time of need.

Hebrews 4:15-16

Yes, I have also experienced a backlash and that is why I do communion and ask Holy Spirit every day of my life to show me all the hidden secrets and evil that is hiding in my brokenness. We all have this, but if you ask Him to show you and take responsibility for it, He will help you to deal with it and forgive you as you repent of it. Then the enemy has no legal right on you. Today I look at prayer differently than before. Prayer opens up a new dimension for us, all through the Blood of Yeshua. Prayer as a petition is part of the judicial system.

Daniel wrote, *"As I looked, thrones were set in place, and the Ancient of Days took his seat. ...The court was seated, and the books were opened"* (7:9a&10c). Satan is continually accusing us before YHVH, and Yeshua is continually interceding for us. We know that these two voices in the heavens are looking for witnesses on earth. Yeshua is interceding for us and declaring blessings over us. He is looking for a witness on earth, someone who speaks Life and declares Life as well. Forgiveness and speaking Life are powerful forces for our Heavenly Intercessor to use. This is a spiritual law.

Reflection:

- If prayer as a petition is part of the judicial system then how much time are you spending in intercession?
- You do not stand alone. You have a High Priest, Yeshua, who stands with you and for you.

Response:

Let us then approach God's throne of grace with confidence.

Love or fear?

There is no fear in love. But perfect love drives out fear, because fear has to do with punishment. The one who fears is not made perfect in love.
1 John 4:18

What methods do you use to get action from yourself or your children? How do you get people to focus; teach someone a lesson; or get someone's attention? What do you do when a problem arises in your home and everything you've tried fails? What works best for you? What do you refer back to? Love or Fear? Emotions are connections binding you to others through joy, fear, love, hate, anger, excitement, guilt, or shame. Our bonds with other people are the emotional connections that help us to meet our needs or the needs of others. All emotions produce either "love or fear." Emotions are exchanged in a home through bonds of love or fear.

Do our children respond to us because they love us or because they fear us? Some children just ignore their parents because they don't love or fear them. They've decided to live in an emotional no man's land. They shut themselves in a place where they are sheltered from any emotions. So many children have fear bonds with their parents. They are so scared to tell the truth. So fearful of the emotional explosion it will trigger that they would rather tell a lie. This is what the system of Baal teaches us—fear! They don't care that YHVH knows the truth about them, as long as their parents never find out!

Reflection:

- Think about the questions posed in this piece—what is your immediate emotional reaction?
- Be honest as you answer each question. Take responsibility for your behavior and your actions.

Response:

Ask YHVH to forgive you for the times you have handled situations with your children badly.

No fear in love

There is no fear in love [dread does not exist]. But perfect (complete, full-grown) love drives out fear, because fear involves [the expectation of divine] punishment, so the one who is afraid [of God's judgment] is not perfected in love [has not grown into a sufficient understanding of God's love].

1 John 4:18 [AMPLIFIED BIBLE]

Yeshua teaches us about the value of love bonds. It is in a way our life support system, like an umbilical cord that binds us together with our Father. This love bond gives us the freedom to live and explore life under His protection and guidance. *I have loved you just as the Father has loved Me; remain in My love [and do not doubt My love for you]* (John 15:9 AMP). The enemy, on the other hand, wants to bind us to him with an umbilical cord of fear where we are too scared to live, express ourselves and be free. The Word tells us that there is no room for both. Fear is no companion of love.

Fear influences our behavior and our thoughts. Fear forces us to keep our focus on the things or persons that hurt us. Our lives become lives of worry and concern; and worry triggers fear. Fear produces long lasting changes and patterns in our minds. It becomes a well-worn pathway for the enemy. It works like a generator that keeps the cycle of worry going. He needs someone in each of our lives who can trigger fear in us and that person becomes the generator for the fear cycle. Fear bonds are used to keep us captive, making us slaves to fear.

Reflection:

- You cannot walk in faith and in fear at the same time. It is one or the other.
- Will you believe Satan and his lies or YHVH and His Truth?

Response:

Declare out loud your choice to walk in faith, love and freedom in Yeshua.

Do not fear

So do not fear, for I am with you; do not be dismayed, for I am your God.
I will strengthen you and help you;
I will uphold you with my righteous right hand.
Isaiah 41:10

The sad thing is that so many children have fear bonds with their parents. People have constant fear of rejection and fears of not being good enough. Fear causes the brain's emotional (or alarm) center (known as the amygdala) to take control and dominate the brain. When this happens, your "will" can no longer control what your mind does. That is how people become controlled by fear. For this to be possible the enemy needs fear bonds. Who better to use than parents who do not walk in love, but control every situation in the house through fear.

Today I want to say to you it doesn't matter how much fear you live in there is always hope! Because Yeshua is saying to us today FEAR NOT! Love motivates, love grows, love sees the best in someone, love picks up, love forgives 70 x7, love is humble, love leaves room for each other's mistakes, love teaches, love listens, love brings joy, love has open arms, love gives, love shares, love overrides the fear centers. Love does not blame others, love does not carry guilt, love does not remember the past trespasses and disappointments, love embraces, love explains and love leads by example. What are the bonds you have with your spouse and your children?

Reflection:
* Do you come from a family where you were controlled through fear?
* Have you dealt with it under Yeshua's blood, or are you controlling your family in the same way?

Response:
Break the cycle today. Using the last paragraph pray all the aspects of love mentioned over your family.

Fruit of fear or love?

But the fruit of the Spirit is love, joy, peace, forbearance, kindness, goodness, faithfulness, gentleness and self-control. Against such things there is no law.
Galatians 5:22-23

Through intense negative emotional experiences strong bonds are formed. These negative bonds are called trauma bonds. Where there are: Anger bonds—people get very angry. Guilt bonds—blame is shifted onto others. Fear bonds—people are threatened. "If you don't, then I will move out… I will leave you… I will divorce you… I will tell everyone…" In our homes guilt-and-fear-punishment is the most common incentives to motivate our children. This is Satan's way of breaking down our children, by programing them with fear. Their trigger will always be worry and this pattern or programing will continue for the rest of their lives until they find the Truth. Intensified fear bonds can ultimately lead people into Satanism (occult) and a life without YHVH.

Hearts become so hard and no love can flow to or from them. These people will have an unteachable spirit. I found that most of these people seek intense music and experiences. They struggle to live a life filled with peace and harmony. They always want to be on a high, living from fear, and controlling others in the same way. Fear becomes like a drug to them. Abusive families use this intense form of fear on children or spouses and call it "love."

Reflection:
- Only YHVH can take our brokenness and shine His Glory Light to heal us again.
- When you are whole you can walk in faith sharing His love and healing with others.

Response:
Ask Holy Spirit to make the Fruit of His Spirit evident in your life for all to see and be blessed by.

His priceless Love

How priceless is your unfailing love, O God!
People take refuge in the shadow of your wings.
Psalm 36:7

My friend, a strong fear bond is not love! I am so sorry, but so many people have the wrong impression of a "love bond." Please ask Holy Spirit to show you what the bonds look like in your family. What are you busy programing? A fear and control bond, or a love bond? Yeshua has only "love bonds" with and for us while Satan works with "fear bonds."

Many people are slaves to fear because that is all they know. I (Retah) came out of a family where we were controlled by fear bonds. I was more afraid of my father than I was of YHVH. I did not understand real love. I was always in fear of not being good enough. And this made me seek acceptance in many different ways. I drove myself to excel and seek acceptance. That was until I met the King, Yeshua. He died for me and loves me with an unconditional love. He never threatens me with fear, instead He always says to me FEAR NOT! I am no longer a slave of fear. I am a child of GOD! When I make mistakes He forgives me. He never judges me, or points a finger at me. He loves me so much that He gave His Son and Holy Spirit to be with me and to help me with everything.

Reflection:

- YHVH says to you today FEAR NOT. He loves you with an unfailing love.
- You can do nothing to earn His love—so just accept it and take refuge in it.

Response:

Thank YHVH that you no longer have to live in fear. Tell Him that you choose to walk with Him in faith.

Draw near in faith

Come near to God and he will come near to you. Wash your hands,
you sinners, and purify your hearts, you double-minded.
James 4:8

YHVH is standing with His hands outstretched; full of blessings, full of life and full of abundance. His face is radiant with love and acceptance. However, to receive all He offers, we need to draw near to Him through faith. There is no other option and there is no other way. YHVH is waiting to bless you, but faith in Him is the requirement. YHVH and all that is within Him awaits us, but we can only enter into this fullness by having faith in Him. We need to travel on the path of faith. It is so simple, but yet also so difficult for those who want to do it in their own strength.

Faith is determined by what we know prior to the event. Faith is pre-knowledge of the coming victory and this knowledge produces peace. Faith is seeing and speaking what He says. It is agreeing with His Word and character. If we know no more than anybody else before the game, then we will be the same as everybody else during the game. Faith is YHVH's Word becoming alive and real to us in a personal way in our challenges. Faith is the result of YHVH declaring the outcome to our hearts through His Word, or Holy Spirit. Believing His Word we know the outcome and accept it as the Truth.

Reflection:

*   YHVH is standing with His hands outstretched; full of blessings—will you accept them?
*   Will you choose to walk by faith trusting that YHVH knows what is best for your life?

Response:

Come near to YHVH and he will come near to you.
This is His invitation to you today.

Faith in action

*Now faith is confidence in what we hope
for and assurance about what we do not see.*
Hebrews 11:1

Many times in the Word Yeshua asks: What do you believe? Why don't you believe? This is because according to your "belief" it is done to you. How do I know what I believe? I have a mental picture, a thought (belief) in my mind, and that is the substance of the things hoped for and the evidence of the things not seen. A mental picture tells a complete story. A mental picture reveals your faith. Some people can tell in detail the whole story of fear, of what they believe is going to happen. And because they believe that it is going to happen, it will.

Do you have a picture of faith? Can you see the picture and the answer? Can you see YHVH's protection over you in these times? Can you? Thoughts need "belief" to make them real. A "thought" becomes a "belief system," and the enemy and YHVH uses only what you "believe." When we think negatively about something or someone, we record the thought and it keeps on playing in our spirit mind. And what is recorded and played will happen to us. The recording can only be erased by the Blood of Yeshua, and then we need to declare and decree a new thought and recording for the spirit mind. A new picture of faith, a declaration of Truth and Faith.

Reflection:

- After everything you have read and been shown are you ready to re-program your spirit mind?
- Do you have the confidence and the assurance of your faith?

Response:

Declare a new picture of faith.
Declare Truth and Faith in YHVH your Father, and Yeshua your Savior.

Ask and believe

"You will pray to him, and he will hear you, and you will fulfill your vows.
What you decide on will be done, and light will shine on your ways."
Job 22:27-28

Faith is not so much something that we have, as something that we do. Faith is believing and then seeing the answer already happening. *My son, pay attention to what I say; turn your ear to my words. ...For they are life to those who find them and health to one's whole body* (Proverbs 4:20 & 22). If His Word does not depart from before your eyes, you are bound to see yourself as Yeshua sees you. Then you will not believe the lies of the enemy. It is because our eyes are not fixed on His Word and His truths that we believe all the fear thoughts.

When we pray, we need to see the answer. You cannot pray in faith with spiritual eyes that can only see defeat? You keep on looking at the wrong things, at the conditions, your situation, the symptoms that make you walk in unbelief and destroy all the effects of prayer. When you pray without faith you will not be able to see a faith result, only the defeat result. *But when you ask, you must believe and not doubt, because the one who doubts is like a wave of the sea, blown and tossed by the wind. That person should not expect to receive anything from the Lord. Such a person is double-minded and unstable in all they do* (James 1:6-8).

Reflection:

* Faith is not so much something that you have, as something that you do.
* *My words. ...are life to those who find them and health to one's whole body.*

Response:

Are you going to choose to walk by faith trusting only YHVH?

Made in the USA
Las Vegas, NV
03 August 2023

75559679R10164